# CONCILIUM

*concilium* 1994/5

# CATHOLIC IDENTITY

Edited by
James H. Provost and
Knut Walf

SCM Press · London
Orbis Books · Maryknoll

Published by SCM Press Ltd, 26–30 Tottenham Road, London N1
and by Orbis Books, Maryknoll, NY 10545

ISBN: 0 334 03028 5 (UK)
ISBN: 0 88344 880 7 (USA)

Typeset at The Spartan Press Ltd, Lymington, Hants
Printed by Mackays of Chatham, Kent

*Concilium*: Published February, April, June, August, October, December.

# Contents

# Editorial: Searching the Meaning of Catholic Identity

How is an institution, a movement, a social teaching, or even an individual 'Catholic' today? It is surprising how frequently this question comes up and how difficult it can be to answer.

Sometimes the question is raised in a polemical atmosphere, as if by denying Catholic identity to the 'other side' it would be possible to win the argument. Efforts to classify a particular position as the only truly 'Catholic' stance have a long history in Christianity, but it is not this dimension of the question which holds the greatest fascination today. Rather, there is a growing concern about what it really does mean to be 'Catholic' in our day. Criteria which once seemed so clear are now in crisis. Practical measures, such as the visible presence of clergy or religious, are becoming less reliable as laity take on a rightful and increasingly visible role in church life. It is to this more fundamental, and pressing, dimension of the question of Catholic identity that we devote this Church Order issue of *Concilium*.

The Second Vatican Council tried to renew the sense of who we are as Catholics by drawing on a variety of concepts: the people of God, a communion of churches, an ecumenically sensitive group of Christians, a witness to the gospel in the modern world. The initial insights of the council have been applied, adapted and modified in the years since Vatican II. The 1983 Code of Canon Law and the 1990 Code of Canons of the Eastern Churches make a contribution to this question; so, too, do various documents from offices of the Roman Curia, and apostolic constitutions from the pope.

Before exploring the practical implications of these developments we present some reflections on the theoretical foundations for establishing Catholic identity today.

Norbert Greinacher leads off with an exploration of the theological background, examining the approaches to Catholic identity at Vatican II and in the post-conciliar period. His synthesis provides a foundation for the canonical considerations by James Provost and Alphonse Borras, who explore two sides of the issue: how church law determines Catholic identity, and the limits to that identity.

Identity is not something abstract; it is culturally conditioned and rooted in time and place. Johannes A. van der Ven addresses identity from the perspective of the local church, while Geoffrey King reflects on the relationship of culture to law and Catholic identity in the specific cultural settings of Asia.

The issue of Catholic identity is posed most acutely in regard to various practical issues. Who speaks for the Church in the media? What does it mean to have 'Catholic' charities in a world where social services are an accepted dimension of government responsibility? How do Catholic hospitals retain their identity in a similar setting? What makes a university truly Catholic, and juridically Catholic? Is there a specifically 'Catholic' manner of providing pastoral care? These are the issues taken up by Ernest Henau, Norbert Mette, John Beal, Roch Pagé and Robert Duggan respectively. Their studies draw on practical experience, careful review of church documents and the conciliar perspective of what it means to be Catholic.

Involvement in ecumenical dialogues, particularly since Vatican II, has provided an important opportunity for Catholics to explain their own identity in a formal but eirenic setting. What is happening in the dialogues, therefore, is an important source for understanding how the Catholic Church is presenting itself today. David Tracy steps back and looks at the general results of this effort from a Catholic perspective, while André Birmelé presents the impressions of a partner in the dialogue.

The results of these studies are both reassuring and unsettling. Catholic identity is being addressed on many fronts; it is not being taken for granted. But are the approaches consistent, or even in sufficient dialogue with one another? Knut Walf's reflections on the future of Catholic identity close this issue of *Concilium*.

We recognize that the topic of 'identity' has a broader application in modern philosophical and sociological studies than we have been able to include here. Our purpose in this issue is to provide our readers with a state of the question and some key principles which we hope will be helpful in addressing Catholic identity in various contexts. In this we seek to provide a reasoned voice to advance the dialogue in what promises to be an ongoing concern not only of church order, but of church people for some time to come.

James H. Provost
Knut Walf

# I · Foundational Considerations

# Catholic Identity in the Third Epoch of Church History

The Second Vatican Council and its Consequences for the Theory and Practice of the Catholic Church[1]

## Norbert Greinacher

### I. The Second Vatican Council as the beginning of an epoch of the world Church

For Karl Rahner the Second Vatican Council represented no less than the beginning of a new era in church history: 'From the theological standpoint, we can say that there are three great epochs in church history, the third of which has only just begun and was authoritatively brought to notice at Vatican II: 1. The short period of Judaeo-Christianity; 2. The period of the Church in a particular cultural group, that of Hellenism and European culture and civilization; 3. The period in which the Church's living space is from the very outset the whole world.'[2]

For Rahner the Council is a caesura in church history of a quality which is paralleled only by the opening up of the Jewish Jesus community to the Gentiles or to the sphere of Western culture. That 'means that the transition from one historical and theological situation into an essentially new one happened only *once* before in the history of Christianity and is now set to occur for the second time in the transition from the Christianity of Europe (with its American appendages) to an actual world religion'.[3]

If Christianity began more than 1900 years ago to change from being a Jewish sect into a great *Western* institution, with the Second Vatican Council the transition to a Church of the *whole world* began: a church which not only defines itself as world-wide in organizational terms but also understands itself as Church in the world, with the world and for the world, with its various peoples and cultures, its pluriform political and economic structures, and its different world-views, religions and confessions.

Purely in phenomenological terms, Rahner's periodization could be interpreted as follows. The Pauline mission and other mission efforts with more of a southern or eastern orientation led first to a 'catholic identity' for Christians, 'catholic' in the sense of 'embracing the whole earth'. In a few centuries Christian communities had come into being throughout the then known world which had links with one another. After the modern age of discoveries it then took almost five hundred years for Christianity, now Catholic in a confessional sense, to discover its new 'Catholic identity': with reference to the world which is now completely known, and which is greater than Europe, North Africa and part of Asia. That would mean that what was epoch-making about the Second Vatican Council is to be seen in a changed consciousness of the modern *quantity* of Christianity.

However, Rahner's argument is a theological one. Thus some church historians will certainly have problems with it. Are Paul (and the first 'Apostolic Council') and the Second Vatican Council the *only* epoch-making events of Christian or confessional Catholic theology and church history? What about the 'Constantinian shift' and the Councils of Nicaea (325) and Constantinople (381)? What about the separation between the Eastern and Western Church in 1054? What about Thomas Aquinas? What about Luther or the Tridentine Counter-Reformation? What about Vatican I?

Rahner understands the term 'epoch' in the same narrow way as the term 'paradigm', which is used in such an inflationary way in more recent outlines of the history of the Church and of theology. Stemming from the scientist Thomas S. Kuhn,[4] in scientific theory 'paradigm' denotes the totality of all the *basic* notions which dominate a discipline in a particular period and thus establishes what can be regarded as a satisfactory scientific solution. So only scientific *revolutions* can be understood as 'paradigm shifts'. Transferred to historical thinking, 'epoch' means something very similar; the much-used or misused term 'epoch' does not denote a *transition* from one *period* (an interval of time characterized by certain events) to another. 'Epoch' denotes a *stopping place* in the calculation of time; i.e. *everything* that has *shaped* the preceding time comes to a standstill, is finally superseded, and something unprecedented, something totally new, begins – as I have said, as a result of the influences which *shape* it.

Paul's actual victory at the so-called Apostolic Council represents such an epoch-making event: it was not just about a changed membership structure of the early church, nor about the transition from a *Jewish sect* to a universal *Church*; as a result of the extension of the Church into the sphere of Roman-Hellenistic culture, faith and the whole of theology, i.e. talk of God, were fundamentally reshaped.

It is very difficult to define a second event in church history as being 'epoch-making' in the sense defined above. Certainly the shift under Constantine fundamentally affected the relationship between Church and state, but not primarily the doctrine of the Church. The Councils of Nicaea and Constantinople are consequences of confrontation with and reflection on the message of Jesus in the context of Graeco-Roman intellectual traditions. The schism of 1054 was above all about church politics, not about the incompatibility of two theological 'paradigms'. Thomas Aquinas merely *re*-discovered Aristotle, and Luther's thought was as late-scholastic as that of his theological opponents; only his conclusions were different. And the First Vatican Council absolutized the absolutist monarchy in the church as a form of rule when this political form of rule was coming to an end.

So between Paul and the Second Vatican Council, i.e. for 1900 years and through many major shifts, the history of theology has moved in at least relative continuity. Does time then stop, suddenly, between 1962 and 1965, for three years, to resume in quite a new and different way?

Put in this acute form, the theory sounds strange, especially to today's younger generation, which has no experience of the time before the Second Vatican Council. Nevertheless it is correct. Today we take all too for granted the changes which the Council stimulated, so for granted that it does not strike us that the second 'paradigm shift' of church history is only thirty years old. Possibly the Council and its pioneering texts would already have been half forgotten, and we would be preparing for the fourth epoch of church history, a council uniting all Christian churches, were not Karol Wojtyla Pope and were not Joseph Ratzinger Prefect of the Congregation of Faith. It is 'thanks' to them above all that the reception of the texts and the 'spirit' of Vatican II progresses all the more intensively, the nearer the next papal election comes.[5]

The controversy over the Council and its spirit is being carried on intensively both by the Roman Curia and by theologians, since the issue is whether the Church risks falling back into the second epoch of its history. The consequences would be unthinkable: a regression of the world Church into a 'world sect', an uncoupling of Christianity and the Church, serious dangers for the transmission of Christian faith generally. That can be prevented today only if the Catholic Church again resolutely follows the texts and the spirit of Vatican II, if these can really develop their power which *shapes identity*.

What is the new element in the Council? What does Catholic identity mean at the Second Vatican Council – *qualitatively*, not quantitatively?

## II.  The Second Vatican Council: two Catholic identities in conflict

Identity means agreement over certain issues and persons. There has never been a Catholic identity that transcends history, nor can there be. Nevertheless, before the Council there was an amazingly comprehensive, at least implicit, agreement among *all* Catholics, men and women, clergy and laity, Magisterium and believers, on what was Catholic. Moreover this pre-conciliar Catholic identity was thought to be unchangeable. No wonder, since after all it was 1900 years old. Otto Hermann Pesch notes the remark of a farmer from the closed, strictly Catholic area of Oldenburg, which indicates the central ambivalence about the calling of the epoch-making Second Vatican Council: the unshakability of pre-conciliar Catholic identity and the sharp sense of the decisive changes under way: 'People in Rome can decide what they like, but I'm remaining Catholic!'[6]

### 1.  The basic features of pre-conciliar Catholic identity

Central here is the doctrine of the Church as *societas perfecta*, which essentially defined the Church at least after Cyprian's (c. 200–258) *extra ecclesiam nulla salus*, though it was only given a full theological formulation by Robert Bellarmine (1542–1621) within the framework of his understanding of the Church and history: the Catholic Church – in its visible, i.e. institutional and hierarchical, constitution – is a 'perfect society' to the extent that in it – and *only* in it – *all* mediation of salvation between God and human beings takes place. Without total *identification* with this Church, without following its values and norms for religious, social and private life down to the smallest detail in everyday life, there is no salvation for men and women, or they are *guaranteed* to be damned eternally. On the one hand this understanding of the Church implies a sweeping condemnation of all men and women outside the Catholic Church – in other Christian churches or other religions.[7] On the other it implies a *certainty* of salvation for all those who obediently claim the Church's structures of mediation: in the light of this ecclesiology Catholic identity would *necessarily* have to be based on complete agreement.

As a result there was an unbreakable connection between the perfect form of the official Church and the perfect form of Christian belief and practice. As far as the praxis of Catholic Christians was concerned, what one had to do or not do was laid down to the last detail. One could read instructions in the handbooks of moral casuistry.[8] For most people of the time the Church had found its perfect form through the First Vatican Council, even if it was impossible to pass a complete dogma on the Church in view of the adjournment of the Council *sine die* because of the world political situation: 'only' primatial authority and the infallibility of the Pope were defined in the constitution *Pastor aeternus*. For the majority of Catholics, however, all the important things had been said about the Church and thus also about faith: *this* Church – and that means in principle the Pope or the church authorities in Rome – proclaims this faith authentically and in an absolutely binding form and would continue to do so authentically and in an absolutely binding form in the future. Though the ecclesiastical authority of the Council was not abolished in so many words, there was widespread assent that the dogmatic statements of *Pastor aeternus* made it unnecessary to pass another; in fact the Council had made itself superfluous.

So we can understand how even in 1958, the year in which the Venetian patriarch Angelo Roncalli ascended the throne as John XXIII, hardly anyone envisaged an imminent council: 'On the contrary, at the time nothing was further from the minds of the men in the Roman Curia, and certainly there was no widespread public opinion within the Church which would have called for one.'[9] When a few months after his election the Pope publicly announced his plan for a council, while his Curia was surprised and irritated, perhaps because it was also annoyed and disturbed at the amount of work which would be involved, it was not really disturbed. Even if in accordance with the Pope's will there was not to be a reconvening and continuation of the (First) Vatican Council, but a second one, people were nevertheless quite sure that it would not, indeed could not, bring *anything new*. If it did anything, it would complete the doctrine of the First Vatican Council with a universal constitution on the Church and make important papal statements of previous decades dogma. The draft texts for the Second Vatican Council were worked out entirely along these lines – down to a draft which wanted to make the immaculate conception of St Joseph a dogma – and there was a firm conviction that these would pass through the council relatively smoothly, as in any case the whole proceedings would be brief, with only one session.

That things turned out very differently indicates that the preparation for and course of the Council had a dynamic of their own; theologically speaking, it points to the working of the Holy Spirit, and above all to the basic mistakes in the Curia's assessment of the position of the world church and the theological convictions of the majority of the bishops who represented it.

Unfortunately it can only be a fancy, but supposing that a Third Vatican Council were to be called and the organs of the Curia prepared the first draft texts for it, and one were to go on to compare the texts finally passed with the first drafts: hardly a statement from the prepared drafts would survive the council.

There is no need to retell the history of the Second Vatican Council here: Otto Hermann Pesch has recently done so in a convincing way. What is important is the fact that during the Council and as a result of the Council there was a hopeless collapse of a Catholic identity which was 1900 years old and supposedly unchangeable: even though the influence of the minority of the council fathers who wanted to hold on to the old was disproportionately strong, they ranged from a minimum of a tenth to a maximum of a quarter of the Council. The overwhelming majority called for a new 'epoch' of church history.

### 2. The basic feature of the conciliar Catholic identity

The Church essentially does *not* consist of its hierarchical structure to which at some point, right down at the broad base of the pyramid, ordinary believers, the laity, also belong – as it were as those who receive commands from the top, without having any say of their own. The Church *is* the people of God, in which *all* believers in principle have equal rights. The ordained ministers (bishops with the Bishop of Rome, priests, theologians, etc.) *serve this* Church on the way through time. So the real basis of the Church is formed of believers, who cannot err in their sense of faith (*Constitution on the Church*, 12).

The Church is not a superterrestrial *societas perfecta*, completely and utterly independent of the realities of the world, above all of the *societas perfecta* of the state. The Church is Church in the world and for this world in the service of the kingdom of God. The Church has to grapple with society, not as something external to it, but as a constitutive element of its existence: as the Church in history and human society.

The Catholic Church is *a* Christian church. There are other Christian churches and church communities which are institutions standing in the legitimate discipleship of Jesus, which are with men and women on the way to salvation.

Christianity is a religion in which men and women can attain salvation (something which does not make the question of truth obsolete but on the contrary enriches it and sharpens it).

All human beings enjoy unlimited freedom of religion and conscience. The question of salvation is not decided with a decision against God or against Christianity.

More obvious consequences of the Council like liturgical reform are subordinate to these central features of Vatican II, which in fact reflect a paradigm shift in self-understanding and in the teaching of the Catholic Church.[10] And questions like the redefinition of the relationship between local bishop, college of bishops and Pope are consequences of the working out of the basic features of the Church.

Taken by itself, what is said about Judaism, which was also felt to be so revolutionary at the time, does not represent a theological paradigm shift for the Church: the relationship of the Church to Judaism was never fundamentally different from the relationship of the Church to *all* non-Christian religions. It was only the *proxmity* to Judaism which provoked a hostility that other religions did not feel in this passionate acuteness. If we regard Christianity as an independent religion, the new conciliar relationship of the Church to religions *generally* comes before its relationship to Judaism: to this degree it is formally a lucky chance that what the Council says about Judaism was ultimately included in a 'Declaration on the Relationship of the Church to the Non-Christian Religions'. In other words, in terms of church history of course the new relationship to Judaism was the paradigm shift, but in terms of the history of theology the paradigm shift was the new relationship to the other religions generally.

So that was the end of the old, familiar Catholic identity which had given Catholics so much certainty and had made the Catholic Church such a closed body. The Church defined itself and Christian faith in a completely new way, both internally and externally. It was the end of the certainty that Catholics and Christians were in a rather better position with God. It was the end of the clear rules of life given from above, which one either had to follow or repent for not following. No, now it was a matter of grappling with secularized society and its interpretations of the world, with other confessions and religions. It was a matter of defining one's own sense of faith instead of having it defined; and one could no longer feel at home in shared expressions of the faith, in worship, but if possible had to make one's own contribution.

Understandably, the feeling of a destruction of Catholic identity was often stronger than the sense of construction. A loss of identity, and the Second Vatican Council certainly represents that, had to be met with the formation of a new, post-conciliar identity. Did the Council also achieve that? I think of the old farmer from Oldenburg: did he 'remain' Catholic, or did he manage to become Catholic again? What does this new conciliar power to form identity look like, if it exists? And what does Catholic identity really mean now? Should it not have long since been sublated –

in the Hegelian sense – into a universally Christian or, to accentuate the issue even more, a transcendent identity? Can we still speak of identity?

## III. Catholic identity after the Second Vatican Council

It was not so easy to make the preconciliar identity disappear, not only in Oldenburg but above all in the Roman Curia. The controversy between preconciliar and conciliar Catholic identity has lost none of its intensity. Since the 1970s, and at the latest since the pontificate of John Paul II (1978), there is talk of restoration in the Church. Restoration in general means the restoration of conditions as they existed before the revolution, and this is precisely what the Roman Curia is attempting with all its power; to reverse the 'revolution' of the Second Vatican Council, or at least to destroy its revolutionary impulses.

In recent years the Roman Curia has sought continually to restore the pre-conciliar identity. It is in this light that for example the reformulation of the *Professio fidei* and the *Iusjuramendum fidelitatis* of 1980[11] and the Congregation of the Doctrine of Faith's *Instruction on the Ecclesial Vocation of the Theologian* of 24 May 1990 are to be seen.[12] This instruction states among other things: 'The Magisterium has drawn attention several times to the serious harm done to the community of the church by attitudes of general opposition to church teaching which even come to expression in organized groups' (32). We may assume that this also refers to the roughly five hundred theologians who signed the 'Cologne Declaration' of 25 January 1989.

The *World Catechism* represented a further attempt on the part of the Roman Curia to restore the pre-conciliar identity.[13] Without observing either the letter or the spirit of the Second Vatican Council, leaving aside the various continents and ignoring the results of theological scholarship, an attempt is made here to define in detail what Catholic faith and morality is: a vain attempt!

That this seems possible shows that a new, post-conciliar Catholic identity has only become partly established. Here the main difficulty is unmistakable and is grounded in the Council itself. Certainly there are statements about the Church as people of God which are well founded in the Bible. But at the same time the Council – as a whole – neglected to undertake a corresponding reform of the institutional Church. What does this new theological definition of Church mean in practice if the real power relationships in the Church have remained the same? What, for example, does the talk of the freedom of theology mean if the use of this freedom is threatened with a refusal of the *Nihil obstat* or a removal of the Church's licence to teach? What is the use of fine words about the non-Christian religions if in principle a marriage between a Catholic on the one hand and someone who is not baptized on the other is invalid in church law (cf. CIC 1983, c. 1086 § 1)? What does the high value attached to the individual conscience mean if the appeal to this conscience is not encouraged, and in cases of doubt there are threats of church stigmatization (cf. e.g. *methods* of birth control, abortion, divorce or remarriage, public acknowledgment of homosexuality)? What is the point of the *de facto* recognition of Christian churches as 'partner churches' if it is still not possible for couples of different confessions to participate together in the same eucharist? No wonder that resignation is widespread in the Church.

A thorough structural reform of the Church along the lines of the theological statements of the Council is an urgent necessity. Without such a structural reform there will be no conciliar Church.

However, many Catholics restrict themselves to calling for changes 'from above'. But that is against both the Spirit of the Council and the praxis of the Roman Curia and many bishops. A conciliar Catholic identity must be formed 'from below'. The people of God are not those who bear the Church in order to allow themselves to be borne by its servants.

I shall now go on to identify some important elements of 'Catholic identity' according to the Second Vatican Council.

1. To be Catholic means to confess the Christian faith in loyalty to the statements of the Old and New Testament, the proclamation of the Magisterium and the historical experiences of Christians: 'The whole body of the faithful . . . cannot err in matters of belief' (*Lumen gentium* 12). 'The fact that the faithful and the Magisterium are mutually dependent on each other, and possibly may even be opposed to each other, is here laid down as a basic fact of ecclesiology . . . There can be no valid magisterial proclamation which is not concerned with believers' awareness of the faith.'[4]

This means that all Catholics have not only the right but the duty to compare their personal faith with the faith as handed down and introduce it into the life of the Church (cf. CIC 1983, c. 212 §2f.).

2. Being Catholic means being part of God's elect and beloved people. But this does not mean exclusiveness. The believers of other churches are also part of this people; our Jewish brothers and sisters have always been there, so their tradition, which in part is also ours, is particularly worth respecting. And in the end all people of all religions and world-views belong to it: 'His [God's] providence, evident goodness, and saving designs extend to all men, against the day when the elect are gathered

together in the holy city which is illumined by the glory of God, and in whose splendour all peoples will walk' (*Declaration on the Relation of the Church to Non-Christian Religions, Nostra aetate*, 1). As Christians we understand ourselves to be, if not on the only possible way, then on a right and true way to salvation to the degree that we follow Jesus of Nazareth. But this way is to be taken with people of other world-views, above all with people of other religions, for there too we find 'what is true and holy' (cf. ibid., 2).

That means that ecumenism within Christianity must be lived out as widely as possible, even in the face of the restrictions of church law: not in a harmonistic way but in fruitful co-operation or juxtaposition of the various confessional traditions. Above all we are firmly to take the path of an institutional reunion of the Christian churches: without such a reunion Christian churches will lose the last remnants of credibility in society.

All non-Christians, and above all Jews, must be encountered in the awareness that they can tell us something about our faith; and we must encounter them with the self-confidence that we can tell them something about true human life and faith. So these encounters must be sought.

3. Being Catholic means being bound up in brotherhood and sisterhood with Catholics throughout the world and not denying the sense of faith of the people of God to any of them, no matter in what culture their roots may be. On the contrary, their valuable contribution to the whole church is to be seen as an essential enrichment.

This means that as far as possible a lively and mutually enriching exchange must take place between the believers of different cultures about their different practices of faith, about their different theologies, spiritualities, liturgical forms, patterns of ministry, etc.

4. Being Catholic means believing that God is active throughout the world, not only in the Church, for this world is God's world.

This means that Catholics must face the challenges of the world and grapple with them and in so doing speak the language of the world: they must passionately make their Catholic contribution to the solution of the problems of the world in society and the groups and organizations which support it.

Granted, Catholic identity has become more difficult to live out since the Second Vatican Council. For first of all it has to be *sought*, certainly within the Christian community, but in the last resort individually, and it must be sought again and again. People were not aware of this before the Council. Being Catholic means being questioned by the world. But in the end – and it is this that constitutes identity – being Catholic can and must also be an enquiry to the world. Being Catholic has become more demanding as a result of the Second Vatican Council, but also more liberating and enriching.

Before the Council, Catholic identity consisted in a total identification with all statements by popes and bishops. Now it has become clear that in the face of the ambivalence of human existence and the possibility that the Church and its Magisterium can err which is bound up with this and has been demonstrated by history, a total identification with the Church is not only impossible, but also inhuman. The result of this is that post-conciliar identity can only consist in a partial identification with the Church.

*Translated by John Bowden*

*Notes*

1. I am grateful to my colleague Mathias Kotowski for important suggestions for this article.

2. Karl Rahner, 'Theological Interpretation of Vatican II', in *Theological Investigations* 20, London and New York 1981, 82f.

3. Ibid., 84.

4. Cf. Thomas S. Kuhn, *The Structure of Scientific Revolutions*, Chicago ² 1970.

5. Cf. Siegfried R. Dunde (ed.), *Müssen wir an der katholischen Kirche verzweifeln?*, Gütersloh 1993; Jakob Kremer (ed.), *Aufbruch des Zweiten Vatikanischen Konzils heute*, Innsbruck 1993; Otto Hermann Pesch, *Das Zweite Vatikanische Konzil. Vorgeschichte – Verlauf – Ergebnisse – Nachgeschichte*, Würzburg 1993.

6. Pesch, *Konzil* (n. 5), 21.

7. The church teaching, following Thomas Aquinas, thought that exceptions were possible only for people who had never come into contact with the Catholic Church and its teaching through no fault of their own but nevertheless unconsciously lived by Christian principles in accordance with their own nature. As soon as there was contact with the Church of whatever kind, other criteria immediately applied. Here a Christian way of life in itself was no longer sufficient for salvation.

8. Cf. Heribert Jone, *Katholische Moraltheologie auf das Leben angewandt unter kurzer Andeutung ihrer Grundlagen und unter Berücksichtigung des CIC sowie des deutschen, österreichischen und schweizerischen Rechtes*, Paderborn 1961.

9. Pesch, *Konzil* (n. 5), 22.

10. Granted, the statements in the Council texts as a rule do not make the point as clearly as is done here and are often unbalanced and contradictory: they are stamped by what Max Seckler has called a 'contradictory pluralism' in order to command the broadest possible (i.e. virtually unanimous) assent from the Council fathers. But it is legitimate to investigate the revolutionary focus of the texts. There are two reasons for that, one external and one internal. Externally, anyone who takes the history of the Council seriously cannot attach the same weight to parts of the texts which were conceded to an ultimately vanishing minority or to the concern of the Pope that the

Council should hold together and be fruitful rather than split apart. Internally, a textual interpretation should always be focussed on the statements which go furthest: for example, if a document formulates the unlimited possibility of salvation for all people (as happens above all in *Gaudium et spes* and *Nostra aetate*), a statement about the necessity of the Catholic Church for salvation (cf. *Lumen gentium* 14) cannot claim the same validity – even if it was passed by the same Council or included in the same document.

11. *Acta Apostolicae Sedis* 81, 1989, 104–6; ibid., 81, 1989, 1169. Cf. CIC 1983 canon 833. The application of the regulation about the confession of faith and oath of loyalty to the sphere of the German conference of bishops has been suspended pending clarification.

12. *Acta Apostolicae Sedis* 82, 1990, 1550–70.

13. Cf. Hansjürgen Verweyen, *Der Weltkatechismus. Therapie oder Symptom einer kranken Kirche?*, Düsseldorf 1993; Ulrich Ruh, *Der Weltkatechismus. Anspruch und Grenzen*, Freiburg 1993.

14. Pesch, *Konzil* (n. 5), 185.

# Approaches to Catholic Identity in Church Law

## James H. Provost

One of the functions of any legal system is to determine the identity of its members, and to provide for the identification of entities within its ambit. Canon law is no exception, and gives consideration to the Catholic identity of individuals, and of groups or institutions which are considered 'Catholic',

### Catholic identity of individuals

There are two systems in present church law for determining the Catholic identity of an individual person. The first is the traditional system based on being baptized a Catholic or received into the Catholic Church, resulting in a Catholic identity which is never lost. The second system is derived from the Second Vatican Council's teaching on 'communion', and recognizes that people are in different degrees of communion with the Church. Are these two systems compatible, or do they produce conflicting results? To determine this, it is necessary to examine each system more closely.

### 1. Baptized or received into the Catholic Church

The previous Code of Canon Law considered anyone who was baptized to be a Catholic because it made all the baptized subject to all the laws of the Catholic Church unless they were exempted for specific cases. Thus Orthodox, Protestants and other Christians were considered 'bad Catholics' but subject nonetheless to the laws of the Catholic Church; i.e., they were identified as Catholics who had gone astray, but were still considered to fall under the umbrella of Catholic Church law.

Present Catholic Church law shows greater ecumenical sensitivity.

Merely ecclesiastical laws (as distinct from divine laws which may also be stated in church law) bind only those who have been baptized in the Catholic Church or received into it.[1] Other Christians are not bound by laws specific to the Catholic Church. This norm has several implications for determining the Catholic identity of an individual.

First, an external rite is necessary to identify someone as a Catholic; it is not enough merely to desire to be Catholic, or to participate in Catholic rituals, or to declare to someone 'I am a Catholic'. Church law makes it clear that persons can be identified as 'Catholics' only if they have received baptism into the Catholic Church, or have undergone the formal rite of being received into the Catholic Church if they were already baptized.

Second, Catholic identity is never lost. A person baptized into the Catholic Church or received into it is always presumed to be bound by Catholic Church law. Even when exceptions from the force of law are made for someone who lacks sufficient use of reason and generally for those who are under seven years of age, or when exceptions are made from specific laws in the Latin Church for those who leave that Church by a formal act,[2] these people are still considered to be subject to Catholic Church law in principle. It makes no difference whether a person becomes inactive, attempts to leave the Church, or even lapses from faith altogether; Catholic law continues to bind them, and thus they continue to remain in some manner identified as a Catholic.

## (a) Baptized into the Catholic Church

What does it mean to be 'baptized into the Catholic Church'? A careful study of the Church's tradition and ritual has clarified that this is not determined merely by the person who administered the baptism, the place or location of the baptism itself, nor even necessarily the ceremony which was used.[3] In an emergency, baptism can be administered by anyone, whether that person is a priest or lay person, Catholic or not, or even Christian or not. For the rite to be valid, all that is needed is that the minister have the intention to do what the Church does, and that the ceremony involve some kind of washing by water and the trinitarian formula: 'I baptize you in the Name of the Father, and of the Son, and of the Holy Spirit.' But whether this rite is baptism into the Catholic Church is ultimately determined by the intention of the person receiving the baptism, or by those who act in that person's behalf (e.g., parents or guardians for an infant).[4]

Normally the intention to be baptized into the Catholic Church is evident from the fact that the person comes to a Catholic parish or other institution, and requests baptism. For adults, going through the Rite for the Christian Initiation of Adults makes it evident that the person intends to become a Catholic. For infants, at least one of their parents or legal guardians must request the baptism;[5] the intention to be baptized into the Catholic Church is evident from their request.

In danger-of-death situations, however, when baptism may take place outside a church setting, determining the intention of the one being baptized is more difficult. Even more complex is the situation of infants in danger of death who may be baptized even against the will of their parents (whether the parents are Catholics or not). This is licit in the Latin or Western Church, but not in the Eastern Catholic Churches.[6] Such an infant is validly baptized; but is the infant baptized into the Catholic Church? Those who are baptized against their will are considered not to have undertaken the obligations of Catholics; the same would seem to apply to infants in these situations, unless later, when they reach the use of reason, they do intend to be Catholics.

The Catholic identity of those who were baptized into the Catholic Church as infants but never raised in that Church is also a problem.[7] Theoretically they remain bound by all the laws of the Catholic Church, even though they know nothing of the Church. If they become members of some other church or ecclesial community, this may constitute the formal act of leaving the Catholic Church which, for Latin Catholics, exempts them from some of the marriage laws; but even then they remain bound by all the other laws of the Church.

Thus the anomalous situation can result that persons baptized into the Catholic Church who have joined another Church or ecclesial community are bound by Catholic law, whereas a non-baptized person who is attracted to the Catholic Church, regularly attends Mass there and otherwise observes Catholic discipline, is not bound by Catholic law.

## (b) Determining which Catholic Church

Baptism into the Catholic Church is always into a specific Church *sui iuris* or what was sometimes called a 'rite'. Once they reach the age of fourteen, non-baptized persons may freely select which Catholic Church – the Latin (Western) Catholic Church, or one of the Eastern Catholic Churches – to join when being baptized.[8] This applies no matter what ritual (Eastern or Western) is used in their baptism; it is their free choice which determines which Catholic Church they join. Usually it will be the Church whose ritual is used in the baptism, but it need not be.

For children younger than fourteen, the rules are more complex. Basically, children are to be baptized into the Church *sui iuris* of their parents; if their parents belong to different Churches *sui iuris*, then they are baptized into the Church *sui iuris* of their father. If their mother is the only Catholic, or if both parents agree, the child may be baptized into the mother's Church *sui iuris*.[9]

Catholics, therefore, are not simply 'Catholics' but 'Latin Catholics', 'Ukrainian Catholics', 'Maronite Catholics', and so on. Their Catholic identity is always further specified in the law, and carries with it definite legal consequences in the Church such as which set of laws are binding, what sacramental practices are to be observed (e.g., with regard to chrismation or confirmation, marriage impediments and their dispensation, rite of marriage, reception of holy orders, etc.), and even the Catholic hierarchy to which they are subject.

The Second Vatican Council re-emphasized the importance of retaining one's rite or Church *sui iuris*. Thus even though for generations a family has practised its Catholic life according to a different Church *sui iuris*, when the children are baptized they are baptized into the Church *sui iuris* to which the parents legally belong (not the one in which they practise). This can lead to some confusion as to what Church *sui iuris* is competent, particularly in areas where populations have become mixed and members of various Churches *sui iuris* can be found. Moreover, the Council decreed that other Christians who come into full communion with the Catholic Church must be enrolled in the Catholic Church *sui iuris* which corresponds to the one of their baptism. Thus Orthodox Christians who are received into the Catholic Church are received into the Eastern Catholic Church which corresponds to their Orthodox Church of baptism, no matter to which Church *sui iuris* the priest belongs who receives them. Similarly, baptized Protestants who are received into the Catholic Church are enrolled in the Latin Catholic Church, even if an Eastern Catholic priest performs the ceremony.

What is the net result of this system of Catholic identity? On the one hand, it is clear who are Catholics: those baptized into or received into the Catholic Church. Usually it is also clear what Catholic Church (Western, or one of the Eastern Catholic Churches) this is. However, given the special cases discussed above, this clarity may be lacking in individual cases. The system is not without its difficulties.

## 2. *Communion*

A second system for determining Second Vatican Council identity derives from the conciliar teaching on communion. Some background is important to understand this development.

The traditional understanding that Catholic identity derives from baptism was modified by Pius XII in the encyclical *Mystici corporis*, where he added that the profession of true faith is needed for one to be truly (*reapse*) a member of the Church. He also explicitly identified the Church of Christ with the Catholic Church. Membership in the Church of Christ, the community of the saved, is by membership in the Roman Catholic Church.

This led to considerable discussion on the question of membership. What, for example, of those who were baptized but did not yet profess the true faith (e.g., infants), or who profess the faith but not in its entirety (those not in communion with the Roman Catholic Church)? Distinctions were made between constitutional membership, which comes with baptism and includes all the rights and duties of members, and the 'active' membership of those who personally assumed the full implications of their baptism. Various levels of belonging to the Catholic Church were explored, ranging from basic human nature through 'anonymous Christians', to spiritual and juridical levels of belonging as a baptized Christian.[10] There were some who took the encyclical to say that non-Roman Catholics are not in the community of the saved, but this proved to be an erroneous reading.[11]

Vatican II addressed these issues with careful nuance. It recognized a distinction between Christ's Church and the organized Catholic Church, although Christ's Church subsists in the Catholic Church. The phrase 'subsists in' was deliberately chosen instead of Pius XII's identifying term 'is' in order to leave some flexibility in evaluating the reality of other churches and ecclesial communions. In effect, instead of making an exclusive statement (Christ's Church and the Catholic Church are one and the same, exclusive of any other ecclesial bodies), the council made a positive declaration of the faith of the Catholic Church that if one is looking for Christ's Church, it will be found here. Whether one might find it elsewhere is neither affirmed nor denied.

With regard to membership or Catholic identity, the Council taught that through baptism one enters Christ's Church. That, however, is not sufficient for full incorporation into the Catholic Church. More is required: 'They are fully incorporated into the society of the Church who, possessing the Spirit of Christ, accept her entire system and all the means of salvation given to her, and through union with her visible structure are joined to Christ, who rules her through the Supreme Pontiff and the bishops. This joining is effected by the bonds of professed faith, of the sacraments, of ecclesiastical government, and of communion.'[12]

The conciliar statement refined the position of the 1917 code with several elements. Full incorporation is distinguished from the immediate effects of baptism: it is possible to be in partial communion, not 'fully incorporated', which would be the situation of baptized persons who do not conform to the conciliar criteria. Conceivably a baptized person can be in some communion with Christ's Church but not be fully incorporated into the society of Roman Catholics.[13]

Translating this teaching into canonical terms proved difficult.[14] The first attempt was in the draft for the *Lex Ecclesiae Fundamentalis*,[15] where several canons dealt with membership from the conciliar perspective. Canon 5 repeated the 1917 code's provision that baptism constitutes one a person in the Church, but modified this by 'the extent to which they are in ecclesiastical communion'. Canon 6 dealt with the qualifications for full communion, drawing on the *Lumen gentium* text above but deleting reference to possessing the Spirit. Canon 7 addressed the condition of other Christians, who were said to be in some communion with the Catholic Church even though this was not full communion. Canon 8 specified that the non-baptized do not belong to the Church, although catechumens have a special status vis-à-vis the Church.[16]

A new canon was drafted for the codes which were promulgated, based on *Lumen gentium* 31 and specifying who are the Christian faithful.[17] It states this in terms of baptism, constitution as the People of God, participation in the three-fold office of Christ (priest, prophet, king), and the call to participate in the Church's mission in the world.

Thus present church law recognizes a two-fold dimension to Catholic identity: first, the basic identity of being a Christian, common to all the baptized; next, specific Catholic identity, which is dealt with in terms of 'full communion' based on the three-fold bonds of profession of faith, sacraments and ecclesiastical governance. There are several implications of these new canons.

First, Catholic identity is based on full communion with the visible society of the Catholic Church. Full communion is verified by the external bonds of profession of faith, sacraments, and ecclesiastical governance. But this also means that Catholic identity admits of the same diversity as these bonds allow. To what extent can Catholics be divergent one from another and still remain in this full communion? One test for this is to consider the degree of diversity accepted by the Apostolic See in such matters. For example, considerable dissent has been tolerated as being within 'full communion' with regard to the central mystery of the Eucharist, particularly in regard to the followers of Archbishop Lefebvre.[18]

Second, from the 'communion' perspective it is possible for Catholic identity to be lost. Elsewhere in this issue Borras argues, for example, that apostasy constitutes a complete loss of visible communion with the Catholic Church, that heresy and schism constitute a loss of full visible communion. These would seem to constitute a loss of Catholic identity, as might also the fact of notoriously abandoning the faith or of leaving the Church by a formal act, which Borras also discusses.

Third, even though the codes do not specify the condition of other Christians (as canon 7 of the *Lex* attempted to do), Catholic Church law does recognize that all Christians in virtue of baptism pertain to the People of God, participate in the three-fold office of Christ, and participate in some way in the mission Christ entrusted to the Church. They are not in 'full communion', but must be in some degree of communion because Christ's Church in whose mission they share 'subsists in the Catholic Church'.[19]

### 3. Comparing the systems

Both systems involve an objective element for a person to have a Catholic identity. For the traditional canonical approach, this is baptism; for the newer, conciliar-based approach, it is baptism plus the external bonds needed for full communion.

Both systems also involve a subjective element. For the traditional approach, this is the intention to be baptized into the Catholic Church (or to be received into it if the person was already baptized). For the newer, conciliar-based approach, in addition to the traditional subjective element there is also the need for subjective intention to continue to be in full communion.

The difference between the two systems appears most clearly in the question of whether Catholic identity can ever be lost. Traditionally, once a Catholic, always a Catholic, even if the apostate, heretic or schismatic was a 'bad Catholic'. For the newer approach, it is possible to lose Catholic identity by breaking the bonds of full communion.

This difference was evident to those revising church law after the Council, but the experts were divided on how to deal with it. Some feared that if Catholics who left the Church were not subject to canon law, they could not be punished for apostasy. Others argued the need for ecumenical sensitivity. Eventually, the final version is sensitive toward those not baptized or received into the Catholic Church, but does not address the anomaly of losing Catholic identity by leaving full communion yet remaining bound by Catholic canon law.[20]

## Catholic identity of groups

In addition to the Catholic identity of individuals, canon law also deals with the Catholic identity of groups and of institutions. Others in this issue of *Concilium* deal with the Catholic identity of specific Catholic institutions, such as charitable works, hospitals, and universities. There are also canons which deal with the identity of Catholic schools[21] and associations of the faithful.[22] Questions have also been raised about the Catholic identity of new movements in the Church.[23]

There are two dimensions to the Catholic identity of groups, institutions, and the like: an internal dimension and an external dimension. Catholic identity requires first of all an inner commitment to being Catholic: observing Catholic teaching, consonance with the mission of the Church, etc. An institution which works at cross purposes to those of Catholics lacks the very inner reality to be considered 'Catholic', whatever its formal title.

Usually an external recognition of this Catholic identity is also necessary. This can be found in the public commitment of the institution or group, or in its recognition by competent church authorities – a recognition given by letter, or in approving the group's statutes, or in the formal establishment of the entity by competent church authority.

Among the issues this approach raises, two are worthy of note here: what criteria are church authorities to use if they are to recognize something as 'Catholic', and is recognition by those authorities always needed for something to have a Catholic identity?

Faced with a proliferation of groups seeking recognition as Catholic, the 1987 Synod of Bishops discussed what criteria should be used in giving this recognition. John Paul II listed five 'criteria of ecclesiality' in his exhortation after the synod: primacy given to every Christian's call to holiness, responsibility to profess the Catholic faith, witness to a strong and authentic communion with the pope and local bishop, conformity and participation in the Church's apostolic goals, and commitment to a presence in human society.[24] These criteria are designed for movements or associations; other criteria may be needed for other kinds of institutions.[25]

Is such recognition required for an entity to have a Catholic identity? The law seems to recognize the possibility of being 'truly' Catholic without such recognition.[26] Many private associations in the Church are *de facto* Catholic, without seeking formal recognition; many predated the categories and requirements found in the revised church law.[27] Their Catholic identity was not questioned prior to the promulgation of the new codes, and should not be a question now.

More significant than a formal recognition of Catholic identity is the responsibility of the hierarchy to exercise vigilance over whoever or whatever claims to be Catholic. This is not only the more traditional manner in which Catholic identity has been safeguarded, it is also the more workable.

## Concluding reflections

The canon law on Catholic identity is not a systematic treatment, neither is it consistent. Various elements were developed for different situations. The law relies on local church authorities to work their way through these differing approaches, and to apply and interpret the canons to individual situations.

This situation points to the need for a better, more consistent ecclesiological foundation for Catholic identity.[28] Perhaps this may be aided by a rediscovered sense of the local church, a perspective which may more adequately reflect the human reality that identity is fundamentally particular and most frequently local.

## *Notes*

1. The norm is virtually the same for the Western or Latin Catholic Church (1983 Code of Canon Law, canon 11) and the Eastern Catholic Churches (1990 Code of Canons of the Eastern Churches, canon 1490).

2. These exceptions are the same ones the 1917 code made for baptized non-Catholics: they are not bound by the Catholic formalities for marriage, or the impediment of disparity of worship, and need not obtain permission to marry a non-Catholic. Cf. 1983 code cc. 1117, 1086, and 1124. The Eastern code has no such exceptions.

3. See Michael Hughes, 'The Juridical Nature of the Act of Joining the Catholic Church', *Studia Canonica* 8, 1974, 45–74, 379–431.

4. Cf. ibid.

5. Latin code c. 868.1, n. 1; Eastern code c. 681.1, n. 2.

6. See Latin code c. 868.2; there is no corresponding provision in the Eastern code.

7. The Congregation for the Doctrine of the Faith issued an instruction in 1980 encouraging the continued practice of infant baptism, but urging careful pastoral care to avoid this kind of situation. See Congregation for the Doctrine of the Faith, instruction *Pastoralis actio*, October 20, 1980: *Acta Apostolicae Sedis* 72, 1980, 1137–56.

8. See Latin code c. 1111.2; Eastern code c. 30.

9. For the rules governing enrolment in a Church *sui iuris*, and subsequent changes in enrolment, see Latin code cc. 111–112, and Eastern code cc. 29–38.

10. See, for example: Klaus Mörsdorf, 'Persona in Ecclesia Christi', *Archiv für katholisches Kirchenrecht* 131, 1962, 345–93; and Bonifac Willems, 'Who Belongs to the Church?', *Concilium* 1 (January 1965), 62–71 [British edition]. Karl Rahner addressed this question a number of times; see 'Membership in the Church According

to the Teaching of Pius XII's Encyclical *Mystici Corporis Christi'*, *Theological Investigations* 2, 1–88; 'Anonymous Christianity and the Missionary Task of the Church', *Theological Investigations* 12, 161–78; 'Observations on the Problem of the "Anonymous Christian"'. *Theological Investigations* 14, 280–94.

11. See letter from the Holy Office to Cardinal Cushing, 8 August 1949, *American Ecclesiastical Review* 127, 1952, 307–11; Denziger-Schönmetzer, 3866–73.

12. *Lumen gentium* 14.

13. For canonical discussions prior to the revision of the code, see: Matthäus Kaiser, 'Aussagen des Zweiten Vatikanischen Konzils über die Kirchengliedschaft', in *Ecclesia et Ius*, Munich 1968, 121–35; Francesco Coccopalmerio, 'La dottrina dell'appartenenza alla Chiesa nell'insegnamento del Vaticano II', *La Scuola Cattolica* 98, 1970, 215–38; Winfried Aymans, 'Die kanonistische Lehre von der Kirchengliedschaft im Lichte des II. Vatikanischen Konzils', *Archiv für katholisches Kirchenrecht* 142, 1973, 397–417; Franz Pototschnig, '"Persona in Ecclesia" – Probleme der rechtlichen Zugehörigkeit zur "Kirche Christi"', in *Ex Aequo et Bono*, Innsbruck 1977, 277–94.

14. See Hubert Müller, 'Zugehörigkeit zur Kirche als Problem der Neukodifikation des kanonischen Rechts', *Österreichisches Archiv für Kirchenrecht* 28, 1977, 81–98.

15. Pontificia Commissio Codici Iuris Canonici Recognoscendo, 'Lex Ecclesiae Fundamentalis seu ecclesiae catholicae universae lex canonica fundamentalis', Rome, 24 April 1980 (*pro manuscripto*); this document was approved by a special commission but never promulgated by the pope. Some of its canons were eventually incorporated in the Latin and Eastern codes.

16. Only two of these canons are repeated in current church law: canon 5, recognizing legal personality in the Church on the basis of baptism (found only in the Latin code c. 96), and canon 6, specifying what is required for full communion. The special status of catechumens is also affirmed, but no mention is made of the status of other non-baptized persons.

17. Latin code c. 204; Eastern code c. 7.

18. Diversity in other respects has also been noted; cf. J. M. Bergoglio, 'Actitudes conflictivas y pertenencia eclesial: a proposito de tres publicaciones', *Stromata* 39, 1983, 141–53, analysing the CELAM documents from Puebla and works by von Balthasar and Barbottin.

19. Ibid.

20. See *LEF* c. 7; *Communicationes* 23, 1991, 151–2; 14, 1982, 132–3.

21. Latin code c. 803; Eastern code cc. 632, 639.

22. Latin code cc. 299–301; Eastern code c. 573.

23. See Jean Beyer, 'Motus ecclesiales', *Periodica* 75, 1986, 613–87; id, 'De motu ecclesiali quaesita et dubia', *Periodica* 78, 1989, 437–52.

24. John Paul II, apostolic exhortation *Christifideles laici*, 30 December 1988, n. 30.

25. See, for example, the standard of education set by Latin code c. 795, Eastern code c. 629.

26. For example, in dealing with Catholic universities; Latin code c. 808.

27. See Roch Pagé, 'Associations of the Faithful in the Church', *The Jurist* 47, 1987, 165–203; Heribert Schmitz, 'Fragen der Rechtsüberleitung der bestehenden kirchlichen Vereinigungen in das Recht des CIC', *Archiv für katholisches Kirchenrecht* 156, 1987, 367–84; Fulvio Uccella, 'Linee di tendenza della disciplina

del fenomeno associativo dal Concilio Vaticano II al nuovo codice di diritto canonico', *Ephemerides Iuris Canonici* 46, 1990, 235–84.

28. See Klaus Lüdicke, 'Die Kirchengliedschaft und die *plena communio*: Eine Anfrage an die dogmatische Theologie aus der Perspective des Kirchenrechts', in *Recht im Dienste des Menschen*, ed. Klaus Lüdicke et al., Graz 1986, 377–91.

# The Communicative Identity of the Local Church

## Johannes A. van der Ven

The title of this article implies a programme. It presupposes that the identity of the local church must not be seen as static but as dynamic, and that it must be realized in communication between all those involved. By local church what is meant here is the church which takes shape in local surroundings at the microlevel. Here my starting point is that it is realized in a dialectical interplay with the church that happens in the national and continental context at a mesolevel and in the intercontinental and world context at the microlevel. However, in this article I am concerned with the local church at the microlevel.[1]

Several aspects of the identity of this church can be distinguished. First of all there is the religious identity. This relates to the religious metaphors and rites and to the religious convictions that these contain. Local churches differ from one another in this sphere. Some parishes recognize themselves in the symbol 'people of God', others in 'community of believers' and yet others in 'religious forum'. Secondly there is the social identity. This relates to the kind of social unity which the local church is and the way in which it is realized. Some parishes are like a hermetically sealed bastion, others like a vital community, others like a network of groups and yet others like a loose association of individuals. So they adorn themselves with different names like 'perfect society', 'family of God', 'association of the faithful'. Then there is the operative identity. This relates to the kind of aim there is, the policy, the programmes and projects that are developed. This is largely dependent on the groups of people who belong to the different parishes. Thus there are typical 'workers' parishes' in which the needs and interests of the workers are the focal point of the management, just as there are also typical middle-class and 'upper-class' parishes. So one can call the parishes 'church of the poor', 'church with the poor' and 'church for the poor'. Finally there is the management identity. This relates to the kind of organization that the local church embodies and the kind of management that sets the tone. Some parishes are characterized by technical-instrumental and financial 'efficiency', others by respect for human relations in the organization, others by a concern for the emancipation and education of their members, and yet others by a concern for innovation and creativity. In other words, parishes differ in openness to the charisms in them and in their pneumatological receptiveness.

In this article I am limiting myself to the religious identity of the local church, and arguing for its communicative development. By this I do not mean that the social, operative and administrative identities need no communicative development. They certainly do! But because of the necessary limitations of this article I can only go into the religious identity here.

At the beginning I already commented on the need to shape this religious identity in communication with all those involved. Here I opted for an approach from above. However important the church leaders' view of the local church is, it is now at last time to pay some attention to the views of the ordinary people who are the subject of the local church. How do they see the religious identity of their church? By what faith do they live? What faith holds them together? What is their perspective on the future? My concern is the 'religion of the ordinary person',[2] the 'religious grammar' of 'native speakers',[3] the 'exoteric language' of ordinary people as opposed to the 'esoteric language' of church leaders,[4] the 'small tradition' in the parishes as opposed to the 'large tradition' of the cultural élite.[5] I shall begin with this 'small tradition', which is laid down in the archives and documents of the official Church and theological libraries. Of course there is an interplay between the 'implicit theology' of the parishes and the 'explicit theology' of bishops and professors.[6] However, there is an asymmetry in this interplay, in which the former is dominated by the latter. So it is necessary to pay special attention to the 'small tradition'.

I have divided this article into three parts. In the first, entitled 'Identity', I offer some insights about the 'bottom up' approach to the religious identity of the local church. In the second, entitled 'Plural identity', I discuss the pluralism which is implied in this approach from below and the conflicts (latent or manifest) connected with it. I shall illustrate this from an investigation that I made in 1990 in some parishes in Ottawa, Canada. In the third part, entitled 'Communicative identity', I shall draw some conclusions from this for church law.

## I. Identity

If one understands the term identity in the traditional sense, communication is superfluous. One does not talk about identity: it simply is, and one knows it. In classical metaphysics the Latin *identitas* indicates the way in which the *substantia* of an entity remains the same despite all the changes undergone by its *accidentes*. The entity is in its being itself and remains itself. It can also be known in this sense. No communication about it needs to take place. In the act of knowing, the human being *qua* human being – any human being – penetrates to this substantial nucleus. This also applies to the identity of the (local) church. The term identity refers – one might say – to the knowable, substantial permanence of the entity, in this case the church.

If we go on to put this substantial identity in a hierarchical-ecclesiological framework, then communication about identity is not only superfluous but even reprehensible. In this framework the identity of the church goes directly back to the divine order of salvation and institution through Christ. It has its foundation in the divine law (*ius divinum*). Further illumination and interpretation of this identity are reserved for the hierarchy of the church, which similarly goes back to divine right. Vatican II certainly pointed to the sense of faith (*sensus fidei*) and the collective consciousness of faith among believers (*consensus fidelium*) as the source of church life, but these are and remain subject to testing by the church's Magisterium (*Lumen gentium*, 12). A 'communication which is free of domination' (in Habermas's sense[7]) about the identity of the local church is the issue in dispute here.

However, this doctrine 'from above' is diametrically opposed to the reality which characterizes the everyday life of a parish. This becomes evident when one looks more closely at the religious identity of the local church on the basis of the facts. I shall do this by bringing out some insights of system theory and applying these to the local church. Some important terms here are: social system, systemic equilibrium, systemic limit, environment and systemic pluralism.

The local church can be seen as a social system to the degree that the members which form part of it interact with one another in a religious sense, undertake common actions in this interaction, and in this interaction and action also cherish emotions towards one another and thus form a single whole. This is what distinguishes the local church from other social systems like the family, the school, the political party, the association, in which different interactions, actions and emotions are involved.[8] The three elements mentioned (interactions, actions and emotions) do not affect all the members of the church equally. In a strictly empirical sense, they apply more to the nucleus than to the modal members; more to the modal members than to the marginal members; and more to the marginal members than the inactive members. Nevertheless, without religious interactions, actions and emotions, the local church simply does not exist.

As a social system it maintains a systemic equilibrium. That does not just mean that there is an equilibrium within the church between the various members and groups in respect of the interactions, actions and emotions, but also and above all that there is an equilibrium between the church and its surroundings. This equilibrum is not to be seen in static but in dynamic terms. It constantly changes as a result of varying influences both from inside and outside, in a reciprocal dialectic. The balance is disturbed when particular groups within the church dominate other groups to a considerable degree and/or certain forces from society have a destabilizing effect on the church. A constant upsetting of the equilibrium poses a fundamental risk to the existence and continuance of the local church.

Thus the church finds itself in an ongoing interaction with its society. In this process it constantly crosses the boundaries between the social system that it represents and its environment. Each time it crosses these boundaries it comes up against the question: where are the boundaries, and can they, may they or must they be crossed and/or shifted? Not only the church leaders are active in crossing these boundaries, but above all the ordinary members of the church. They have to fulfil various functions and roles in the other social systems in society with varying interactions, actions and affects. The systemic limits indicate what can, may and must be brought into the church and what cannot.

So the fundamental question is how the church as a social system interacts with its environment. It can (attempt to) behave as a closed system when it is afraid that the influence from its environment will endanger its religious identity. It then cuts itself off from the existential convictions, values and norms which exist outside the church, and it sets up high thresholds for participation in church and liturgical life. It can also behave (or attempt to behave) as an open system and make itself receptive to new ideas, new movements and new initiatives from its environment.

In the perspective of system theory it is not church government alone which defines religious identity in an authoritative way, but the ordinary members of the church, who, in their everyday crossing of frontiers, in fact realize this identity with their social environment. Here of course there is a fundamental pluralism. Depending on the various social systems in which members participate and the differing degrees to which they identify with them, they introduce different convictions, values and norms into the church, and with them also different priorities. These different convictions cannot just be mutually complementary, but also contrast and conflict with one another. The systemic pluralism in the local church can thus develop into systemic conflicts.

In addition, local churches differ from one another because they are set in different contexts, by which they are influenced in different ways. This insight is one of the attainments of postmodernism, in which modernity reflects upon itself critically. Social systems – including the church – are to be regarded as contextually defined constructions in a particular space and time which are subject to processes of deconstruction from other contexts – 'decontexts'. This makes them reflect upon themselves and criticize themselves.[9] In principle syncretism is simply to be regarded as the result of the contextually defined processes of interchange between the local churches and their varying contexts and criticism of syncretism as the result of a negative evaluation of them from another context.

## II.  Plural identity

If we want to describe the content of the pluralism of religious convictions which relate to the identity of the local church, we are constantly dogged by the question of which convictions form part of the identity and what priority there is among them. Are all convictions equally important?

One can introduce either a material or a formal hierarchy. With a material hierarchy there is the danger that it will itself become a pattern of conflict. For example, does 'faith' have a higher theological status than 'hope'; 'creation' a higher status than 'liberation'; or 'orthodoxy' a higher status than 'orthopraxy'? One can opt for a formal hierarchy in order to avoid such a discussion. One example of this can be found in Parsons' theory of culture and religion.[10] This theory states that four different formal levels are to be distinguished in convictions relating to cultural or religious identity: ultimate reality, ultimate order, spheres of life and activities.

I shall now illustrate the religious convictions which relate to these four levels, using as an example some findings from a survey of five parishes in Ottawa, Canada, in 1990.[11]

Convictions about ultimate reality answer the question what the deepest ground is of the reality in which we live, and which the relevant institution represents. The deepest ground of a culture can be the nation, the sense of 'us', or the language. For a religion the deepest ground is transcendence, and for Christian religion the deepest ground is the God who has manifested himself in Jesus. So here I shall first present the convictions of the Ottawa parishes about God and Jesus as indicated in the survey.

It emerges quite clearly that there is a pluralism of convictions about God.[12] Regular churchgoers seem to believe firmly in God, but in so doing they differ from the official teaching of the Church. They make no distinction between belief in God as personal and belief in God as impersonal. They have no difficulty in moving between personal and impersonal images of God. Moreover they seem to differ from the marginal members and the dormant members of the Church. Despite some doubt, these last maintain a more or less immanentist, pantheistic image of God, which regular churchgoers must have nothing to do with.

There also seem to be different convictions about the significance of Jesus.[13] In the official teaching of the Church the emphasis is always put more on christology coming from above than on christology from below. However, the church volunteers in the survey who support the Church in their spare time seem to attach considerable significance to the man Jesus, his love for his fellow human beings and his 'Abba' God, even more so than the non-volunteers in the parishes.

Convictions about the ultimate order are a response to the question whether the social reality which in fact exists needs to be continued or altered on the basis of faith. Is the existing situation seen as cosmos which needs consolidation or as chaos which needs reshaping?[14] Is social inequality accepted or rightly criticized on the basis of the evangelical symbol of the Church of the poor? The most committed believers among the parishioners in Ottawa have a very critical attitude to existing society, whereas those whose belief is less strong have doubts about the need for social reform. The same applies to the parishes which in fact find belief important for their everyday lives. They think that society needs reform, finding their faith less important, and tend to have more of a doubtful or negative attitude towards it.

Convictions about the spheres of life relate to the degree to which on the basis of faith people attach significance to particular values in, for example, the sphere of personal life, the family, professional life, recreation.[15] To begin with the sphere of personal life: whether the parishioners believe strongly or not, or whether they find faith more or less important for their daily life, does not affect the degree to which they can see being able to take decisions in their personal life (autonomy) as an important value. Moreover, it is notable that parishioners evaluate this autonomy in a negative way. I know from another investigation that people who do not go to church and are not religious clearly always value this autonomy (much) more highly. Often religion and autonomy are in tension. As for the sphere of the family, in general, parishioners in Ottawa to some degree doubt whether it is really important for them to be married, to care for their children and to have a family life (familialism). However, there is a clear difference between those who believe strongly and find faith important for their daily life and the other parishioners. The first group finds this familialism important, but the second clearly has doubts about it. As for professional life, no differences are to be noted in religious terms. The degree of religious feeling or church commitment is irrelevant when it comes to the question whether having a career or getting a good salary is important (economism). Everyone seems to think this important. However, the parishioners who are employed attach a greater significance to economism than those who have no work. This is remarkable, because one often comes across the idea that economism increases as a value among those who have no work. How does that finally relate to the sphere of recreation? In general, parishioners thought pleasure and enjoyment (hedonism) important. There do not seem to be any differences governed by religion or the Church. However, younger parishioners and those who have work find this hedonism more important than the others.

Finally, convictions about activities put these in a particular religious and church perspective. Let us look more closely at the group of church volunteers. They form a third of the parishioners surveyed in Ottawa. They are engaged in every possible kind of liturgical, catechetical, pastoral, missionary, diaconal and administrative activity. More clearly than the rest of the parishioners they think that the monocratic, hierarchical structure of the Church must be broken through in the direction of democracy. They are clearly also more oppressed by it in their voluntary activities. Here they have a fundamental conflict (whether latent or manifest) with the church leadership. Furthermore, they agree with the other parishioners that the Church needs to be open to the ideas of the surrounding culture and that it must lower or shift the threshold for participation in church life. Here too there is a fundamental conflict (whether latent or manifest) with the church authority which has spread from Rome throughout the world. The volunteers who engage fully with the Church and devote their spare time to it are the ones who are most strongly opposed to it.[16]

The only possible conclusion from all this is that the religious identity of the local church is to a considerable degree marked by pluralism and by conflicts (whether latent or manifest) entailed by this pluralism. This applies to the religious convictions about ultimate reality (God, Jesus), ultimate order (social equality and inequality), the spheres of life (autonomy, familialism, economism, hedonism) and activities (volunteers with an open mind in a closed Church).

## III. Communicative identity

The phenomenon of pluralism in the local church necessitates the making of a choice. There are three possibilities. The first option is to put one's head in the sand and avoid the conflicts (whether latent or manifest) which pluralism entails. I am not being cynical, but my empirical perception indicates that this often happens among church leaders, pastors and voluntary workers. The reason is that conflicts, above all in a normative organization like the (local) church, are often evaluated in such a negative way that those who bring to light a conflict that has long been dormant are themselves regarded as the disrupters of unity. As a result, the blame for the conflict is readily foisted on them and they are the ones who have to bear the burden of it – one-sidedly. Conflicts which in fact could be seen to be constructive are often re-garded as destructive because of the fear of conflicts and of the danger of escalation and disintegration. In fact all this issues in ecclesiastical evasion, with the result that things get covered up. This results in administrative negligence and neglect. The local church, with all its tensions, is usually left to its fate.

The second possible option is to establish the content of the religious identity from above, in a hierarchical line. The purpose of this is to maintain or to restore consensus in the (local) church. The conflicts which are in fact present or threaten to arise are silenced from above. This approach, which is also applied in other organizations, is known as hierarchical conflict management. It is usually adopted in combination with two other approaches: structured consultation and external media-tion. Together these three approaches comprise a whole arsenal of methods of regulating conflicts which can and must be used alterna-tively when there are conflicts in organizations. However, in the Church almost exclusive use is made of the hierarchical approach. Rules of structured consultation which apply when conflicts occur are almost completely absent from church law. Rules of external mediation attach very little importance to an independent third party. If there are con-flicts in the Church and they are not denied or avoided, they are usually resolved in a hierarchical direction, at least if this can be called a resolu-tion.[17]

The third possible option is to use the methods and techniques of

communication. This is really the only adequate approach. The pluralism of religious convictions that permeates religious identity everywhere
cannot be denied, nor can it be silenced by decrees from above. It calls
for the realization of a process which has three phases: reciprocal
exchange, understanding on the basis of a reciprocal exchange of
perspective, and the forming of a consensus.[18] The phase of reciprocal
exchange consists in giving in two directions information about notions,
convictions and ideas (cognitive); experiences, feelings and attitudes
(affetive); efforts and intentions to act (conative). The phases of
understanding come about because the persons concerned are not just
communicating with one another from the perspective of their own
selves but also adopting the perspective of the other and arriving at a
co-ordination of perspective on the basis of this exchange of perspective.
The phase of consensus-forming consists in the effort to arrive at a
general or at least partial agreement. To the extent that this agreement
has not been reached, the aim is at least an 'agreement about disagree-
ment'. These three phases have a taxonomic order. In other words, the
aim of the second phase cannot be achieved unless the first phase has
gone through fully, and the aim of the third phase has not been reached
unless the conversation partners have gone through the second phase.
Two different styles of communication are to be combined in these
phases: arguing, to the degree to which the convictions contain values;
and bargaining, to the degree that they imply interests.[19] The arguing
aims at convincing (not overriding) the other on the basis of good
arguments which can be advanced on behalf of the particular conviction. These arguments can be exegetical, historical, systematic and
empirical. The negotiation involves finding a compromise that comes as
close as possible to a solution acceptable to all concerned. Such a
compromise is to be legitimated theologically from the eschatological
perspective of the approach of salvation from God, in which there is a
tension between 'already' and 'not yet'. If the tension is abandoned, one
ends up either in the 'already' of ecclesiological fanaticism which
destroys the Church or in the 'not yet' of ecclesiological cynicism which
equally leads to the disintegration of the Church. The making of such
a compromise finds ethical legitimation in the notion of *prudentia*.
*Prudentia* does not mean discretion, but understanding. According to
Aristotle, it is *the* method of household management.[20] According
to Thomas it is a strategical and tactical concept which holds together
ideal and reality.[21] We can learn from Troeltsch what compromise
implies from the concept of *prudentia* in the ethical-ecclesiological
sense: insight into the relativity of one's own position, tolerance and

respect for that of others, and the provisional character of compromise.[22]

Now in what sense is all this important for church law? I take from
the jurist Knut Walf the insight that a sober consideration of actual
reality in the study of church law is necessary in order to arrive at a true
evaluation of current church law in the light of the plausibility structure
of today's society.[23] This plausibility structure is directly opposed to
the hierarchical regulation of conflicts which is employed almost exclusively in the Church. The application of this form of regulation in a
church in a democratic society does not diminish the existing conflicts
but increases them: it adds power conflicts to the opposition between
monocracy and democracy.

In addition to the general insight into the structure of the Church I
want to bring out an insight which relates to the parish. According to
canon 515 a parish is a particular community of Christians at the local
level. Canon 204 describes who Christians are. Christian are those who
are incorporated into Christ, made the people of God, by baptism. In
the next canon, canon 205, it is said that Christian believers belong
fully (*plene*) to the community of the Church, and are bound to Christ
by three bonds (*vincula*): the confession of faith, the sacraments,
and church government. Canon 209 sets out what this bond implies,
stating that Christian believers are always obliged to remain in
communion with the Church, but fulfilling with great scrupulousness
the duties to which they are obliged, both of the Church as a whole and
of the particular church. The nub of the problem which arises here
from the perspective of the communicative identity of the local church
relates to church unity and the three bonds. First of all there is the
dynamic interpretation of full (*plene*) membership of the church community as expressed in *Lumen gentium* 14, replaced in canon 205 with a
static view.[24] Secondly, the bond of *diakonia* is lacking, though it is
expressed in the formula *una optio, una grex*.[25] Further, the bonds
mentioned are put in one line, as if the bond of church government had
the same status as that of the confession of faith and the sacraments.
Finally, the nature of the bonding expressed by these bonds is formulated in terms of obligations towards the Church. My objection is that
the hierarchical 'narrowing' which takes place here implies a limitation
of the different ways of regulating conflicts which I described earlier,
and is directly opposed to the necessary communicative conception of
unity and community which is necessary for our society and our time.
The religious identity of the local church in a society and a time in
which church membership is based on the individual's own, free,

decision simply consists in the mode of communicative identity. One can ask whether otherwise this does not run the risk of becoming a legal fiction.

*Translated by John Bowden*

## Notes

1. J. A. van der Ven, *Ecclesiology in Context*, Grand Rapids 1994.
2. J. H. Kamstra, 'Een moeilijke keuze: de godsdienst van de gewone man', *Tijdschrift voor Theologie* 20, 1980, 3, 253–79.
3. G. A. Lindbeck, *The Nature of Doctrine*, Philadelphia 1984.
4. R. Schreiter, *Constructing Local Theologies*, New York and London 1984.
5. P. Burke, *Popular Culture in Early Modern Europe*, Aldershot 1978.
6. P. Berger, *Zur Dialektik von Religion und Gesellschaft*, Frankfurt 1973.
7. J. Habermas, *Theory of Communicative Action* (2 vols), Oxford 1985, 1988.
8. G. C. Homans, *The Human Group*, New York 1961.
9. A. Giddens, *The Consequences of Modernity*, Cambridge 1991; S. Toulmin, *Cosmopolis: The Hidden Agenda of Modernity*, New York 1990.
10. T. Parsons, 'The Dimensions of Cultural Variation', in T. Parsons et al. (eds.), *Theories of Society*, New York 1965, 964–71.
11. I am grateful to Dr E. King and Dr A. Visscher of St Paul University in Ottawa for their help in organizing this survey. The reason why the findings in this article differ from those in the paper 'Congregational Studies from the Perspective of Empirical Theology' (in M. Pelchat, *Empirical Approaches in Theology*, Université Laval, Quebec, Canada 1992, 101–30) and in my *Ecclesiology in Context* (n. 1), is a different statistical treatment of the missing values. For further information refer to the author.
12. We measured belief in God with the relevant instrument from A. Felling et al., *Religion in Dutch Society*, Steinmetz Archive 1987.
13. For more information about the instrument with which we measured the significance of Jesus see my article (n. 11).
14. We derived this instrument from Felling, *Religion* (n. 12).
15. We derived this instrument from Felling, *Religion* (n. 12).
16. To measure the monocracy/democracy in the church and the cultural openness of the church and its low structural level we used the relevant instrument from R. Jeurissen, *Peace and Religion*, Theologie en Empirie, Kampen and Weinheim 1993.
17. A. H. M. van Iersel and M. Spanjersberg, *Vrede leren in de kerk*, Serie Theologie en Empirie 18, Kampen and Weinheim 1993.
18. J. A. van der Ven, *Practical Theology. An Empirical Approach*, Kampen 1993, 50–1.
19. J. Habermas, *Faktizität und Geltung. Beiträge zur Diskurs-theorie des Rechts und des demokratischen Rechsstaats*, Frankfurt 1992.
20. Aristotle, *Nicomachean Ethics*, VI, V.
21. Thomas Aquinas, *Summa Theologica* II–II, 48, 50.
22. V. Drehsen, *Neuzeitliche Konstitutionsbedingungen der Praktischen Theologie* I–II, Gütersloh 1988, I, 586–612; van der Ven, *Ecclesiology* (n. 1).

23. K. Walf, *Kirchenrecht*, Düsseldorf 1984, 20.

24. P. Krämer, 'Die Zugehörigkeit zur Kirche', in J. Listl et al. (ed.), *Handbuch des katholischen Kirchenrechts*, Regensburg 1983, 62–71.

25. L. Boff, *Church, Charism and Power*, New York and London 1985.

# Identity, Law and Culture

## Geoffrey King

I am writing these lines in my native land, Australia, during a few weeks away from the country where I live, the Philippines. It is Christmas time, and it feels very different from Christmas in the Philippines. Here there is no novena of Masses at dawn, no groups of carol singers coming round to the house, of course I hear no Tagolog carols, and I will miss the splendid Tagolog settings of the Gloria at the Christmas Masses. The seasons are different – the dry cool season in Manila, summer in Sydney, the days there at their shortest, here the dawns early and the twilights long. In Sydney the carol singers are replaced (a happy innovation) by buskers on the city streets, the songs one hears include carols from the Australian 'bush', and the combination of liturgy, family celebration, the beach, the cricket Test on Boxing Day has a rhythm of its own. Filipino Christmas piety seems to an Australian highly sentimental. Australian piety is so austerely understated as to seem non-existent to a Filipino. We share, fortunately, the same narratives from Matthew and Luke, the same Advent poetry from Isaiah, but we hear them (I suspect) and respond to them (I know) very differently. I feel here, as in Manila, both at home and not at home.

In both places at Christmas our two identities, Catholic identity and national identity, become inextricably mixed. Filipino Catholic identity is not the same as Australian Catholic identity. We are different people, with very different histories. Catholic identity is, inevitably, shaped by culture.

This is a small instance of the principle, well known to theologians of inculturation, that culture is not like a set of clothes that we put on. Culture is part of our body, not our clothing. We are necessarily inculturated beings. Gospel and Church too are inevitably inculturated, even if we have sometimes taken certain forms of Western Christianity as if they were some kind of culture-free essence.

Many popular conceptions of culture, and some official church references to it, do seem to follow the 'set of clothes' model. We are thought to be inculturated if we incorporate some local colour into the liturgy – prayer shawls instead of chasubles, local gestures of reverence, the Bible enthroned among bird of paradise feathers. All of these things are admirable, but they only touch the surface. If inculturation ends there, we fall into the trap of believing in a pure (un-inculturated) gospel that has simply to be expressed in ways intelligible to different peoples, a pure (un-inculturated) church order that requires simply minor adaptations to suit local conditions. And there is the danger of equating culture simply with art, music, dance and the like. That brings a further danger of thinking of culture as the 'high' culture and not the 'popular' culture.

A much more profound notion of inculturation has been espoused by the Federation of Asian Bishops' Conferences. At their first plenary assembly (Taipei, 1974) they called for a threefold dialogue – with cultures, with religions and with the poor.[1] This is really a way of explaining three aspects of a single dialogue, since most Asian cultures are profoundly religious and since most Asian people are poor (despite, and partly because of, the recent much publicized economic boom in several Asian countries). The bishops recognize that culture is not simply art; it is the way a people lives together.

Moreover, the bishops call for dialogue. Real dialogue requires openness to change, to conversion. A church that really dialogues risks becoming transformed in the process. Hence, the challenge goes far beyond 'making intelligible' or adding local colour.

Finally, the bishops talk about these dialogues as beginning in a 'dialogue of life', a sharing in the lives of ordinary people. Inculturation is not simply a task of experts. It happens when ordinary people come together to face the issues most important in the life of their community, issues that sometimes involve threats to life. More recently we have come to talk about forming basic human communities. In this sense, inculturation is not a goal to be deliberately pursued. If people are really involved together in the struggle for life, and if Catholics bring to this struggle the riches of their faith tradition, then that tradition will 'automatically' become inculturated.[2]

All this poses considerable challenges for a church law which deals with structures of community, structures of governance, liturgical celebration, resolution of conflict, the shaping of so basic an institution as marriage and family, the administration of property, and a whole range of symbols of Catholic identity. The challenge is particularly acute for a codified church law, since a codified law is a strong form of legislation 'from above' or from the centre, whereas the model of inculturation that I have proposed comes definitely 'from below' or from the margins.

Vatican II, however, seems to encourage us to meet precisely that challenge in *Lumen gentium* 23:

> By divine Providence it came about that various churches, established by the Apostles and their successors in various places, in the course of time coalesced into several groups, united organically. These groups of churches, while preserving the unity of faith and the single divine constitution of the Church, enjoy their own discipline, their own liturgical usage, and their own theological and spiritual patrimony . . . This variety of local churches with a single inspiration manifests very splendidly the catholicity of the undivided Church. In a similar way, the conferences of bishops today may work together in many and effective ways so that the collegial spirit may be brought to concrete application.

We know well the vicissitudes of interpretation and implementation to which that paragraph has been subjected. It has been taken to refer only to 'rites' and then applied even to them in quite restricted ways. The 'single divine constitution of the Church' has been taken to be an extremely detailed affair. 'Local church' has been taken to mean exclusively diocese (or equivalent) and then diocesan autonomy has been 'defended' in such a way as to reinforce Roman centralization. The *collegialis affectus* has been treated as some kind of vague feeling far removed from the 'effective ways' and 'concrete application' of the text.

But if we take the text at face value, it encourages precisely the kind of inculturation that I described earlier. It is not about adaptation of a pre-existing text, but about the incarnation of the Gospel in a particular place, organic growth in a local context, growth into a distinctive disciplinary system, liturgy, and theological and spiritual patrimony.

The process of restrictive interpretation and implementation is most obvious in the post-conciliar treatment of episcopal conferences. *Lumen gentium* 23 saw them as a contemporary expression of the groupings of local churches so evident in the first millennium, a contemporary expression of the principle of synodality. In the early stages of revision of the Code of Canon Law this insight was given partial expression. But even this partial expression was severely curtailed in the later stages of the revision and in the final text.[3] What we are left with is the possibility of bishops and bishops' conferences making minor adaptations to an already closely defined structure, or of conferences legislating in matters where some national uniformity is thought to be desirable (such as clerical dress (CIC 284), the norms for training of deacons and priests (CIC 236, 242), the setting of a minimum age for liceity of marriage (CIC 1083 §2), establishing a national catechetical office (CIC 775 §3)).

But the closely defined structures remain. With regard to the sacrament of penance, for instance, both the diocesan bishop and the bishops' conference are given roles in determining whether the conditions for general absolution are present (CIC 961 §2). But this within a framework which treats general absolution as only for serious emergencies and individual confession as normative. There is no possibility for bishops devising, for example, a sacramental rite for reconciliation of disputes within a community, where it would be precisely communal not individual confession that would make sense.

A further difficulty comes from the requirement that many of even these 'minor adaptive' decisions must have confirmation or approval by the Holy See. This has caused considerable frustration in the area of liturgy.[4] Only one significantly new eucharistic rite – that of Zaire – has been developed and approved. Even though it remains considerably dependent on the Roman *Ordo Missae*, its approval demanded enormous persistence (during a nineteen-year process) on the part of the bishops. Indian adaptations – concerning gestures, postures, and some minor re-structuring of the rite – has not yet received definitive approval. The 'Mass of the Filipino People' has remained in some Roman limbo for about eighteen years, even though it contains some quite conservative elements and many of its 'adaptations' could be justified simply by applying traditional principles of canonical interpretation. As a result, it is little used.

Of course, our legal texts are not lacking in recognition of the law's limitations and need for adaptation. *Sacrae disciplinae leges* asserts the primacy of love, grace and charisms, and sees conciliar ecclesiological teaching as the pattern to which the Code must be related.[5] The last word of the Latin Code (CIC 1752) put the 'salvation of souls' as the supreme law: the ultimate good of people is more important than any of the preceding 1,752 canons. The same canon demands equity not literalness or harshness. The rules of interpretation tell us to interpret the law in context and to take account (at least where the meaning of the law is doubtful and obscure) of the law's purpose and circumstances (CIC 17). There is broad (and underemployed) scope for dispensation from disciplinary laws (CIC, cc. 85–93). Privileges can be sought (CIC, cc. 76–84). A variety of cases are left to the discretion of local office-holders. Not a few laws contain exceptive clauses, which allow for adaptation to circumstances. Application of the adage *de minimis con curat praetor* can help us see the forest rather than the less important trees.

Many of these aspects of the law go too frequently unrecognized. They are particularly necessary in a codified system of law. Taken together they are a great help to the avoidance of canonical fundamentalism. This is especially true of the directive towards the purpose and circumstances of the law. Many 'difficult cases' can readily be solved by using these time-honoured principles. But in the context of the two codes they remain at the 'minor adaptation' level. They presuppose a fixed law, and allow it to be used with some flexibility and even creativity. But the context is not that of law entering into dialogue, and perhaps being utterly transformed in the process. Even less is it the context of laws emerging 'from below', out of the shared life-struggles of people, from the 'dialogue of life'.

Yet our canonical tradition does contain precisely one such element of a law 'from below', the recognition of custom. The Latin code continues to call custom the 'best interpreter' of laws (CIC, c. 27), even if it allows a contrary custom to acquire the force of law only in the most severely restricted of circumstances. It is obvious that even this limited possibility does open the way to regional variations. The related matter of reception of law can operate in a similar way. As late as the eighteenth century commentators saw non-reception of law as possibly a sign that the law lacked *utilitas* for the place where it was not received. Germany provided the stock example: if laws on, for instance, fasting were not observed there, it was because conditions in Germany (presumably in the wake of the Reformation) were very different from those in Italy.

Custom has, however, potential to operate in more radical ways. Much of written law, after all, developed out of the practice of the community. The Eastern Code, happily, seems open to such a broad vision: 'The custom of the Christian community, as it corresponds to the activity of the Holy Spirit in the ecclesial body, may obtain the force of law' (CCEO c. 1506 §1).

What emerges from the 'dialogue of life' can surely be seen as custom of this kind. The dramatic changes which have taken place in the sacrament of penance can be seen as the product of such a dialogue with cultures. The early form of the sacrament, reconciliation with the community of one who had committed a serious crime, clearly makes sense in the context of a close-knit community where membership was more a matter of choice than of socialization. Not surprisingly its decline coincides with Christianity's becoming the religion of the majority. The second form, as exemplified in the Irish Penitentials, arises from a mixture of monastic desire for spiritual direction and the need of potentially anarchic tribal societies for means of social control. Again, it is not surprising that this form fell into decline as tribes coalesced into the beginnings of nation states and as a new social grouping, the town, came into existence. The third form, individual confession, had a special appeal in this new 'urban' society, and formed one stand in the immense cultural shift from emphasis on community to emphasis on individual which took place in twelfth-century Europe. At different stages in this process both church councils and individual clerics lamented and even condemned the changes that were taking place, but custom in fact prevailed over written legislation.

The history also enables us to see that individual confession, for all its value, was made to bear pastoral burdens for which it was not designed. For centuries it was the only form of individual pastoral care available to the great majority of Catholics. Hence, issues needing something like family counselling had to be squeezed into the format of confession of sins. Given that in some cultures other forms of pastoral care are now rather readily available, it is not surprising that the practice of individual confession has fallen away. (Of course, there are other factors operative – the guilt-inducing way that the sacrament was often 'celebrated', changed attitudes to authority and personal responsibility, changed understandings of sinfulness, and more.)

At the same time we are coming to see more and more the need for other celebrations of forgiveness and reconciliation – reconciliation of disputes within a community, a process for reintegration into the faith community of people who have drifted away from it, acknowledgment of participation in sinful structures. Such forms of celebration are in fact developing in different parts of the Church, even if some of them do not need the canonical requirements for sacramental validity. They may well be the contemporary equivalent of the penitential practice developing in Ireland in the early Middle Ages.

In very significant ways too the discipline related to indissolubility of marriage has been shaped by cultural and social factors. The famous compromise of Alexander III on the significance of consummation of marriage came only after the Church had lived for centuries with the Roman tradition (with its focus on *consensus*) and the Germanic tradition (with its focus on *copula*). In effect, the compromise was a recognition of the validity of two customary usages, which in turn grew out of two very different cultural contexts and different sets of cultural presuppositions. The sixteenth century bulls *Altitudo, Romani pontificis* and *Populis et nationibus* represent an accommodation to the new situations of polygamy and the slave trade that the Church encountered as it moved into the Americas, Africa and Asia. The 1924 Helena case and the subsequent development of other 'privilege of the faith' cases come from a comparatively new situation of inter-faith marriages, and exemplify a readiness to let pastoral instinct prevail over cast-iron theory. In these cases theory for the most part followed practice.

The development of the understanding of marriage consent that made possible the great increase in declarations of nullity in the past twenty-five years has come in response to such social/cultural shifts as the shift of emphasis from extended to nuclear family, significant increase in life expectancy, recognition of the dignity of women, changing expectations with regard to marriage, the development of the human sciences (especially psychology and sociology), increased social and geographical mobility. The response came not precisely as customary law, but definitely as law 'from below', in this case from the jurisprudence of the marriage tribunals, which only subsequently was codified.

The last set of changes are predominantly cultural shifts within generally 'Western' culture. But the whole history of marriage consent must encourage us to ask questions emerging from other cultures, for instance, those where it is not consent or consummation that makes the marriage, but the birth of a child. Or from cultures where polygamy seems to be compatible with permanence, fidelity (polygamy is not promiscuity), and the proper upbringing of children.

It is again a commonplace that structures of church governance were shaped by secular models of governance and attendant cultural presuppositions. Schillebeeckx has argued that the mono-episcopate arose in the cultural context of Roman Asia Minor, with its preference for one-man rule.[6] Less controversially, it is recognized that the structure of diocese and parish was 'borrowed' from the governmental system of the late Roman Empire. The Roman centralization that began with the reforming popes of the late eleventh century are part of a process of centralization (exemplified for instance in Henry II of England) taking place in European 'states' as well as in 'church'. Cause and effect are not easy to distinguish here, but the inculturated nature of the changes in church governance can hardly be questioned.

This history naturally prompts Catholics living in Western-style democracies to ask whether democratic elements cannot be incorporated into church structures. It may also prompt those in other cultures to ask whether their local elements might not also be incorporated. To take but one example. It is prescribed that various councils, such as the parish pastoral council and diocesan pastoral council, are 'merely consultative' bodies. The notion of 'merely consultative', or the distinction between consultative and deliberative, seems to make sense primarily in situations where issues are resolved by voting. But some Asian and African people avoid voting. A decision emerges, in ways perhaps baffling to an outside observer, from a process which may involve telling of stories, moving the discussion apparently tangentially, taking account of the opinions of absent people. At no moment is any vote, let alone a merely consultative vote, taken.

Women in various parts of the world have likewise drawn attention to the cultural limitations of many decision-making structures in both church and civil society. Such procedures tend to be adversarial, creating winners and losers; they place almost exclusive emphasis on logic, forgetting the importance of symbol, story, relationship. The proposed alternatives can bear considerable resemblance to the Asian and African models alluded to above. Again, they may render irrelevant distinctions between consultative and deliberative.

Practically speaking, in the Asian context the dialogue of life, the growth of custom leading to new structures of community and governance is likely to occur in basic ecclesial (or, in some countries, basic human) communities. In places with which I am familiar, like the Philippines or Indonesia, these are not seen as an alternative to parish or diocesan structures. In most places, basic communities are simply subdivisions of the parish, offering the possibility of more genuine experience of community, more opportunity for sharing of prayer and of faith-experience, sometimes at least encouraging greater involvement with social issues. But when taken seriously throughout a diocese they have produced significant structural changes – new kinds of relationship between clergy and laity, diocesan policy-making assemblies more flexible and especially more representative than the diocesan synod, decision-making structures which by-pass (as indicated above) the deliberative/consultative dichotomy, new kinds of ministry of the Word. As a result, some dioceses are drawing up from their experience new organizational charts, not contradictory to any significant points of the code, but looking rather different from the picture that the code seems to draw.

Some of the customs I described earlier took centuries to have their effect. Basic communities are at most a few decades old. What they need is encouragement, not premature legislative limitation. With such encouragement they may play a large part in leading to the goal hoped for by many Asian Catholics, to be part of a Church not just in Asia but of Asia. Custom emerging from culture and entering into dialogue with the traditions of the wider Church can lead, in Asia and beyond, to the forging of an identity which is no longer foreign yet also truly Catholic.

## Notes

1. G. Rosales and C. G. Arevalo (eds.), *For All the Peoples of Asia: Federation of Asian Bishops Conferences Documents from 1970 to 1991*, Maryknoll, NY, 1992, 14–16.

2. Discussed eloquently and extensively by Aloysius Pieris, *An Asian Theology of Liberation*, Maryknoll, NY, 1988.

3. See, for example, Thomas Green, 'The Normative Role of Episcopal Conferences in the 1983 Code', in *Episcopal Conferences: Historical, Canonical, and Theological Studies*, Washington 1989, ed. Thomas J. Reese, 137–75.

4. Frederick R. McManus, 'The Possibility of New Rites in the Church', *The Jurist* 50, 1990, 452–6.

5. John Paul II, Apostolic Constitution (promulgating the 1983 Code of Canon Law), 25 January 1983: *Acta Apostolicae Sedis* 75/2, 1983, xi.

6. E. Schillebeeckx, *The Church with a Human Face*, London, 1985, 124–8.

# The Canonical Limits of Catholic Identity: Some Problematical Situations

## Alphonse Borras

To interpret the law of the Church necessarily entails taking seriously the particularity of the *sui generis* society which is the Church. That is all the more important in such a difficult and extremely delicate subject as demonstrating the canonical limits of Catholic identity, in particular in problematical situations. Neglect of a theological understanding of Christian experience, both personal and ecclesial, can lead to deep misunderstandings in the process of interpreting the *letter* of the Code.

Christian existence is an existence which has taken the risk of faith in the God who has come to encounter human beings. It is demonstrated by confident commitment and the practice that it induces. 'Come and see' (John 1.39,46). In this respect, faith is the beginning of a journey: 'we walk in faith,' writes the apostle, 'not by sight' (II Cor. 5.7).

Through baptism, believers have become members of the Body of Christ. But they are *fully* incorporated into Christ and the Church only if they live fully by the Spirit of Christ (*Lumen Gentium* 14b).[1] In this respect, the Church is a people of believers *on the way*. It is *not yet* at the end of its journey: it is aware of the distance which separates it from its hope. A sign and a pledge of the gathering to which God summons all people, the Church is not made up *of everyone*, but it is there *for everyone*. In human history, its condition is that of being on the way.[2]

The Church is an extremely heterogeneous reality: in addition to the great legitimate diversity of vocations, charisms, ministries (*Lumen gentium* 32) there is the sinful condition of its members: *ex maculatis immaculata*, as St Ambrose wrote (*In Lucam* I.17). This age-old conviction is basic to our topic. The Church is called on to keep fellowship with Catholics in a 'problematical' situation. This fellowship will certainly prevent it from settling down with a good conscience. At all times it will remind itself that faith is a risk, the beginning of a journey: 'We have been saved, but in hope' (Rom. 8.24).

Faced with different personal situations which are problematical from the point of view of Catholic identity, the Church cannot claim to make a final judgment on the *salvation* of these individuals. It does not have the right to do so: *de internis non iudicat Ecclesia*.[3] God alone is *judge* (Ps. 50.6; Matt. 3.12; 7.1; Luke 3.17; 6.37, 41; Rom. 2.1; 4.4, 14; I Cor. 4.4–5; James 4.12; etc.). The Church can only take note of a problematical situation, state *objectively* that it is contrary to the Christian vocation of the Catholic concerned, and say how *in principle* this situation endangers the evangelical coherence of the Church's testimony, specifically the vocation of all its members to holiness.

## I. Catholics in a state of manifest grave sin

Sinners form part of the Church.[4] Through its liturgy, in particular its penitential practices, the Church reveals and realizes the need, and thus the obligation of Christians, to pray for sinners but also, in the end, to work for their own conversion. So the Church's relationship to sinners is not an external one, as if they were an extrinsic reality (cf. *Lumen Gentium* 8b).

However, Catholics who have committed a grave sin are not members in the same sense and the same fullness as those who live in the grace of justification. They are not *fully* incorporated into the Church (*Lumen Gentium* 14b). The grace of baptism remains real, but it does not unfold in their lives in all its fruitfulness.

*Grave* sin essentially has three canonical effects. The first is the prohibition of communion without prior sacramental confession (c. 916).[5] From the beginnings of the Church, grave sinners were judged *unworthy* to approach the eucharistic table for communion in the sacrament of the new *covenant* (II Cor. 11.27–28). Their separation from eucharistic communion is based on a threefold demand for personal authenticity (not *lying* to oneself), coherence in one's Christian life (not *playing* with the sacraments) and the credibility of the Church's witness (not *contradicting* this witness). The second canonical effect of grave sin is the obligation for the sinner *to confess* before being able to take a full part in the mass through eucharistic communion (c. 988, cf. also c. 989). The third effect is for the sinner to be incapable of gaining indulgences (c. 996 §1).

The Code envisages other effects of grave sin when this sin is *manifest*, in other words, when the gravity of its imputability is quite public. According to canon 1184 §1.3° (in the strict interpretation, cf. c. 18), unless they have given some signs of repentance before their death, *manifest* grave sinners are to be deprived of Christian funeral rights if celebration of these rites is likely to cause public scandal among the faithful. So it would have to have been seen that there was *no* sign of penitence on their part and the risk of *public* scandal would have had to be considered (in cases of doubt cf. c. 1184 §2). If moreover the Catholic obstinately persists in his or her grave manifest sin, the Code instructs the minister of communion not to admit them (c. 915) and the minister of the anointing of the sick not to confer this anointing on them (c. 1007). So it would be necessary to prove the occurrence of the gravity of the sin, its manifest character, and the persistence and obstinacy of its author. Note that the legislator has taken care to distinguish between obstinacy and simple persistence. In case of legal doubt, i.e. about the scope or sphere of the application, the minister is not bound by these dispositions (cf. c. 14).

## II.  Catholics under penal sanctions

Penalty implies a delict. One can only make the object of a penal sanction someone who has committed a delict, namely a morally wicked act seriously imputable to a person on the basis of the deliberate violation of a law or a precept (*dolus*, malice, cf. c. 1321 §§1 and 2) for which a penal sanction is provided. That is the notion of delict that can be deduced from canon 1321 §1. In principle, only an act committed by reason of malice (*dolus*) is open to being punished; anyone who has committed an act by culpability, i.e. by omitting the requisite diligence (*culpa*, cf. c. 1321 §2), is not the object of a penal sanction (*non punitur*, c. 1321 §2). Moreover, in principle only the act for which a penal sanction is provided by a law or a precept is punishable, i.e. is open to penal sanctions (c. 1321 §1). However, it can be that in the absence of any provision for a penalty, a particularly grave violation of a law may call for a penal reprisal (*punitio*) or that the need to warn against or to make good the scandal demands it (c. 1399). So in Church law the legal principle *nullum crimen, nulla poena sine lege* is not applied in all its rigour.[6]

The canonical notion of delict thus implies a morally evil act. In other words, speaking theologically (*theologaliter*), the delict implies a grave sin (cf. *graviter imputabilis*, c. 1321 §1). So every delict is a grave sin but not every grave sin is a delict. In principle, only grave sins qualified as delicts (cf. cc. 1364–1398) are open to penal sanctions. The penalty provided can be optional or obligatory, determinate or indeterminate. For example, abortion is punished by a determinate penalty, excommunication is punished *latae sententiae*, i.e. the punishment is incurred by the very fact of the offence (c. 1398). By contrast, membership of an association which plots against the Church is punished by a penalty which is indeterminate (by the Code, but the judge will determine in each case, c. 1374).

The Code lays down the circumstances which do not make a wicked act a *delict* and which as a result exclude any penalty (c. 1323). For example, the minor of less than sixteen who has an abortion is not committing a delict *strictly speaking* (c. 1323.1) even if, objectively, her act constitutes a grave sin for which she must be examined unless her moral responsibility is diminished. Since the author of the act is not yet sixteen, she is not committing any delict and absolutely must not be subject to *penal* sanctions (*nulli poenae est obnoxius*, c. 1323).

The Code also expressly lays down circumstances which temper the imputability of the offence and consequently carry with them a diminution of the penalty or possibly the replacement of it with a penance (c. 1324, §1; cf. c. 1340 §1). For example, for a minor of sixteen or seventeen, age is a mitigating circumstance (1324 §1, 4°). Similarly, ignorance of the penalty also tempers the imputability of the act and diminishes the penalty provided for (c. 1324 §1, 9°). As a reminder, these mitigating circumstances, like all the others listed in canon 1324 §1, rule out any application of a penalty *latae sententiae*. Thus for example a person of age who has had an abortion in full awareness and with complete consent but who was ignorant that abortion is to be punished by an excommunication *latae sententiae* does not necessarily undergo this penalty provided for by the Code.

Generally speaking, canonical penalties can be understood as supplements to penance, *aggravationes paenitentiae*, which punish the refusal of the author of the offence to take seriously the question of *his or her* conversion and reparation for his or her act. All the penalties have a twofold aim, the correction of offender and reparation for his or her crime (cf. c. 1341). So-called *remedial* punishments or *censures* – excommunication, interdict and suspension (cc. 1331–1333) – principally aim at the amendment of the guilty party: their purpose is essentially remedial (or corrective) but at the same time expiatory (or, better, as reparation). Once the guilty party has repented and his or her amendment is attested in a reparation appropriate to the offence, the censure *must* be remitted (c. 1358 §1 cf. c. 1347 §2). So-called *expiatory* penalties (cc. 1336–1338) are aimed directly at the reparation of the act. Their specific aim of reparation is not necessarily accompanied by a remedial or corrective aim (cf. CIC 1917 c. 2286).

Canonical penalties have legal effects which entail a *limitation* of the canonical condition (cf. c. 96). This limitation will vary depending on the penalty incurred or imposed and the way in which it is applied (c. 1312 §1 and c. 1314; c. 1343; c. 1347 §1; cf. c. 1352). In principle censures must be remitted in the external forum (cc. 1354–1360) before the author of the delict (hence of a grave sin) can receive sacramental absolution (c. 916; cf. c. 1331 §1,2° and c. 1332; c. 1352). Censures *only* deprive the guilty party of the capacity to exercise (*capacitas agendi*) certain rights of his or her patrimony. Thus a person who is excommunicated is deprived of the capacity to exercise a number of rights according to the terms of canon 1331: excommunication in no way withdraws the capacity to enjoy (*capacitas iurium*) these same rights. Expiatory penalties, by contrast, deprive a person of the capacity to enjoy certain rights which would thus disappear from his or her legal patrimony. To analyse the limitation of this canonical condition it is necessary to distinguish not only the capacity for enjoyment and exercise but also the different levels of legal patrimony affected by it. The first level is that of the fundamental rights and duties of the baptized (c. 204 §1; cc. 208–223). These rights derive from baptism (cf. c. 96). They are consequently inalienable; *only* their exercise can be limited, indeed suspended. The second level is that of the subjective rights and correlative duties attached to a particular state, *status*. The rights and duties of the lay state can be the object of a deprivation of the capacity to exercise them but not of the capacity to enjoy them (but one *loses* the lay state only by entering the clerical state). The rights and duties of the clerical state are inalienable as far as the capacity of enjoyment is concerned, given the indelible character of the sacrament of order; however, the capacity to exercise them can be lost (cf. cc.290, 292). The capacity both to exercise and to enjoy the rights and duties of the consecrated state of life can be lost (cf. cc. 684–704; 726–730; 742–746). The third level consists in the totality of facts and legal actions which have had and still have determinative effects on the legal action of the person in question, for example obtaining an ecclesial office (cc. 145f.). One can not only deprive someone of the rights and duties which are attached to him (cf. c. 1131 §1, 3°; c. 1333 §1, 3°) but also remove the titular person from office (c. 196; c. 1336 §1,2°).

The limitation of the canonical condition of the Catholic who is punished under law is expressed in a restriction of his or her participation in the life of the Church. This restriction depends on the effects of the penalty in question and the form in which it is applied. The number and importance of these effects vary considerably between the effect of excommunication *ferendae sententiae* (c. 1331 §§1 and 2; c. 171 §1, 3°; c. 316; c. 915; cc. 996 §1 and 1109) and deprivation of an honorific title (c. 1336 §1, 2°) or even between the effects of an interdict *latae sententiae* (c. 1332, cf. c. 1331 §1.1° and 2°) and dismissal from the clerical state (c. 1336.5°). The same goes for the participation in the life of the Church that these penalties consequently bar: whereas the one who has been deprived of an honorific title can as it were take the same part in the life of the Church as before suffering the imposition of this expiatory penalty, the person who is excommunicated *ferendae sententiae* is deprived of the spiritual benefits of the Church to the degree that he or she can only take part in a very limited way in the life of the Church. It should be said in passing that the rigorous analysis of the effects of excommunication in no way allows one to conclude that the person excommunicated is excluded from the Church. He or she has not ceased to be a member of it; his or her capacity to exercise several rights and duties is only suspended until amends have been made.

The Catholic under penal sanction remains a member of the Church even if he or she is *less fully* incorporated into it by virtue of the sin inherent in his or her offence and the refusal of the penitential approach which has given place to this *aggravatio paenitentiae* represented by the canonical penalty.

### III. Catholics who have become apostates, heretics or formal schismatics

Three delicts deserve special treatment because of their consequences for the Catholic identity of their author: apostasy, heresy and schism (c. 751 and c. 1364 §1). These delicts are obviously a matter of strict interpretation (c. 18).

Apostasy is 'the total repudiation of the Christian faith' (c. 751). It can only be the act of someone who has been baptized, not of a catechumen, precisely because it presupposes baptism. It is principally a sin against the faith: in fact it consists in refusing to continue to recognize God, Father, Son and Holy Spirit, as Lord of history, creator of the world and sole saviour. Consequently it brings about the total rupture of the *tria vincula* – the three bonds of the profession of the faith, the sacraments and the ministry of the Pope and the bishops – and puts its author outside *visible* communion with the Catholic Church (cf. c. 205).

Heresy is 'the obstinate post-baptismal denial of some truth which must be believed with divine and catholic faith, or it is likewise an obstinate doubt concerning the same' (c. 751). The negation or the doubt must be obstinate, *pertinax*: it is not enough for the intelligence to deny or doubt. It is not enough for it to be mistaken. In addition, what is necessary is a resolute, obstinate, opinionated will to deny or doubt a truth which has been formally revealed, whether explicitly or implicitly, and is contained in the one deposit of faith entrusted to the Church (*DS* 3011; *DV* 310; c. 750). In no case can this be a truth virtually revealed, i.e. a simple theological conclusion deduced from a truth formally revealed, even if this conclusion seems evident or has been defined by the Church. Heresy puts in question the *vinculum symbolicum*, the bond of the profession of faith, and by this doctrinal course the *vinculum sacramentorum*: it puts its author in a less full visible communion with the Catholic Church (cf. c. 205).

Schism is 'the refusal of submission to the Roman Pontiff or of communion with the members of the Church subject to him' (c. 751). It is not the absence of communion as such with the Pope or with one or more members of the college of bishops in communion with him, but the refusal, *detrectatio*, to put oneself in such a relationship which constitutes the offence of schism. Schism must be *direct*: the refusal of communion must be the object *directly* willed and sought by the will. If the break in communion is an indirect consequence of another act which is the main and direct thing willed, there is no schism in the sense of canon 751. For example, a particular Church wants to change the rites of the sacraments or the discipline of ecclesiastical celibacy without consulting the universal Church or the See of Rome. Its direct concern and aim is to change these rites or this discipline, and not the break, which, if it came about, would only in this case be the indirect consequence of the change in question. Nor should schism and disobedience be confused. The latter is a simple transgression, for example, of pontifical laws; the former is a deliberate and voluntary refusal of communion, and thus a rebellion. The inherent sin in the offence of schism is a sin against charity, more particularly against an effect of charity, its most sublime, namely the unity of the Church. Schism provokes a rupture of the *vinculum hierarchicum seu communionis* – the bond of communion – and puts its author in a less full visible communion with the Catholic church (cf. c. 205).

To be seriously imputable (c. 1321 §1), the delicts of apostasy, heresy and schism must be deliberate and voluntary, but also external and *completed* in the terms of canon 1330, namely perceived by a third party. It will be noted that the *external* character of the offence is not identical to its *public* character, which, in the case of delicts, denotes the *divulgation* (cf. CIC 1917 c. 2197, 1° and 4°). Here *public* is opposed to *occult*: an offence is occult when by its necessarily external character it is known by certain people but has not been obligatorily divulged more widely in the community. *External* character is not identical to *notoriety*, in law or in fact (CIC 1917 c. 2197, 2° and 3°), which does not denote the simple divulgation of the delict but the (re)cognition of its imputability.

For the delicts of apostasy, heresy and schism, canon 1364 stipulates excommunication *latae sententiae* and, if relevant, the applications of canons 194.§1, 2° and 1336 §1, 1,° 2° and 3°. Given the difficulty of specifically discerning these delicts in reality and pronouncing on them with the greatest legal certitude, it would have been better to provide a penalty *ferendae sententiae* for them.[7] The Code lays down yet other sanctions for these two crimes, depending on well-defined objective or subjective circumstances (c. 149, §1; c. 171, §1,4°; c. 316; c. 694 §1,1°, cf. cc. 729, 746; 1041, 2°; c. 1044, 1, 2°; c. 1071, §1,4°; c. 1086, §1; c. 1184, 1,1, etc.). If committed by clergy, these delicts, if they are *public*, entail an irregularity in exercising the orders which have been received (c. 1044, §1,2°). *Notorious* apostates, heretics and schismatics – i.e. those of whose imputability there is no doubt – must be denied ecclesiastical funeral rites unless they have given some sign of penitence before their death (c. 1184 §1,1°).

### IV. Catholics who have defected from the faith or the Church in a public or notorious way

Not all Catholics who have rejected the Catholic faith or defected from the communion of the Church in a *public* (c. 194 §1,2°; c. 316) or *notorious* (c. 171 §1,4°; c. 694 §1,1, cf. cc. 729 and 746; c. 1071 §1,4°) way necessarily come into the triple category of Catholics who have become apostates, heretics and formal schismatics (c. 1364 §1, cf. c. 751). Here the strict interpretation is *de rigueur* (c. 18). In canons 194 §1,2° and 316, the rejection of the Catholic faith or defection from the communion of the Church is *public* – as opposed to *occult* – when it is known by all, or at least by many people, i.e. widely in the community: in other words, the rejection or the defection is public when it is *divulged*.

In canons 171 §1,4°, 694 §1,1° and 1071 §1,4°, the term *notorious* simply means *known* and does not have the technical sense that it has in penal matters (namely 'the imputability of which is in no doubt', cf. CIC 1917 c. 2197, 2° and 3°). Several arguments demonstrate this. First of all the context and the matter of these canons are not penal but purely disciplinary. Then canon 167.4° of the 1917 Code spoke of those who are members of or adhere *publicly* to a heretical or schismatic sect, which does not necessarily mean that these persons had become heretics or schismatics. Canon 646 1.1 of the former Code spoke of *public* apostates from the Catholic faith. Canons 171, §1°,4° and 694 §1, 1° now use the adverb *notorie* where the previous Code spoke of a *public* act. In the case of canon 1071 §1,4°, which has no parallel in the former Code, the majority of commentators continue to interpret *notorie* as 'in a way known (by all)'. Here the term cannot have an exclusively penal sense ('of the imputability of which there is no doubt'); it is only after an examination of the situation by the local Ordinary that the latter can *possibly* conclude apostasy or formal heresy (c. 751, cf. c. 1364 §1) and, should it be that the other person has not been baptized, exempt them from the canonical form (c. 1117).

*Public* or *notorious* defection from the faith or the Church does not necessarily imply a grave imputability or the obstinacy which are the mark of the delicts of apostasy, heresy and schism. The defection must have been the object of a more or less *implicit* will to leave the Church (otherwise one would have to include non-practising members). This defection can be the result of the absence of an awakening to faith or Christian education, ignorance of the matter, indifference, spiritual laziness and so on. Certainly there is some responsibility among Catholics who have 'become unbelievers', but there is perhaps also a lack of boldness, fervour and support from Christian communities in which in principle these Catholics should have blossomed and come to an adult faith.

## V.  Catholics who have defected from the Church by a formal act

By contrast, defection from the Catholic Church by a formal act implies the expression to a third party of a will no longer to be a Catholic or no longer to be considered such. Here the adjective *formal* is opposed to *virtual*, which denotes the expression of the will of a subject through an action which results from the force (*virtus*) of his or her will as much as he or she reflects it.[8] Defection from the Catholic Church by a formal act presupposes the full knowledge and entire consent of its author. It is a grave imputable action. Each case should be examined to see if the conclusion of apostasy, heresy or schism is an appropriate one. That will be relatively easy when the Catholic has defected from the Catholic Church to join another Christian confession, a non-Christian religion or other religious groups commonly called *sects*, like for example Jehovah's Witnesses. It will be equally easy when the Catholic defects from the Church and professes an atheistic or agnostic doctrine. In all these cases membership of another group or adherence to another doctrine *as such* constitute the formal act. The evaluation will sometimes be more delicate when it is a matter of defection pure and simple: here the criterion of the formal act will be the declaration – the *declared will* – of the interested party that he or she no longer wants to be recognzied as a Catholic. One thinks, for example, of requests to be deleted from the baptismal register.

Once they have defected from the Church by a formal act, Catholics are no longer subject to the canonical rules in the case of marriage with an unbaptized person. Canon 1086 §1 exempts them from the impediment of disparity of cult. This is a new development in comparison to canon 1070 of the 1917 Code. The explanation is that this impediment, the aim of which is to protect the faith of the baptized person, no longer has any *raison d'être* for a Catholic who has left the Church. Correlatively, canon 1117 exempts the latter from the canonical form if he or she contracts marriage with someone who is not baptized. Similarly, canon 1124 gives exemption from its prescriptions for marriage with a Christian who is not a Catholic.

## VI.  Catholics in an irregular matrimonial situation

When conjugal cohabitation, *convictum coniugale*, becomes impossible in practice, canonical legislation accepts the separation of the partners if there is a legitimate cause like adultery (c. 1152), a grave spiritual or physical danger for the spouse or the children, or extreme difficulty in living together (c. 1153). Canon 1152 refers to adultery as a cause for perpetual separation. In other cases, the legitimate causes for separation give rise, at least generally, only to a temporary separation: the separation ceases and cohabitation must be restored, at least as a rule, when the legitimate cause of separation comes to an end (c. 1153 §2).

In numerous present-day civil legislations, after a few years legal separation results in civil divorce. In this case there is no moral fault by the partner who had a legitimate reason for separation because he did not seek divorce directly. Civil divorce is not always a moral fault and, for example, the innocent partner in a civil divorce does not contravene the moral precept (*Universal Catechism*, nos. 2383, 2385).

Canonical legislation ignores civil divorce, even if it takes note of certain canonical consequences of civil marriage which would have ended in failure and possibly in divorce (c. 1071, §1,3°; cf. c. 1093). It only considers a few cases of the canonical dissolution of the marriage bond (cc. 1141–1149).

The 1983 Latin Code of Canon Law, later than the apostolic exhortation *Familiaris consortio* of 22 November 1981, did not take up expressly the refusal to admit to eucharistic communion divorced persons who had remarried in a civil ceremony 'who have made themselves incapable of being admitted because their state and condition of life is in objective contradiction to the communion of love between Christ and the Church as this is expressed and made present in the eucharist' (no. 84d). The *objective* description of their situation should be noted, a description which does not necessarily exclude taking seriously different subjective situations (no. 84b). The 1992 *Catechism* notes a 'considerable difference' between two extreme situations – the innocent partner unjustly abandoned who is the victim of the divorce and the partner who is gravely responsible for a divorce (no. 2386, which moreover refers in a note to FC 84). One may ask whether implicitly this does not suggest taking seriously *less* considerable differences. At all events, there should be no economizing with moral and pastoral discernment. *Familiaris consortio* already required pastors to take good note of different situations 'for a love of the truth' (no. 84b).

With the benefit of these considerations we can analyse the disposition in canon 915. This is directly addressed not to the faithful but to the ministers of Holy Communion and stipulates that they are not to admit to eucharistic communion, among others, 'those who obstinately persist in manifest grave sin'. It will be easily understood that the minister of communion can only pronounce in the external forum and is not necessarily capable of appreciating in the internal forum the gravity of the sin and the obstinacy of the sinner. Certain canon lawyers think that canon 915 relates to divorced persons who have remarried in a civil ceremony, basing themselves on the preparatory works and referring to *Familiaris consortio* (no. 84d).

However, it will be noted that the Code does not give apostolic exhortation as the authentic source of canon 915. Moreover, there are reasons for asking about the scope or sphere of application of canon 915: there is doubt as to whether or not the case of divorced persons who have remarried in a civil ceremony falls within the scope of this canon. *Lex dubia lex nulla*. There is a legal doubt, and according to canon 14, *lex non urget*. Moreover, it can easily be realized that one cannot know for certain whether or not any given case of divorced persons who have remarried in a civil ceremony falls within the framework of canon 915. So in practice there will very often be factual doubt. Quite apart from the subjective imputability of a situation which is *objectively* sinful (cf. FC 84d), its gravity, its manifest character, its perseverance and the obstinacy of its authors would have to be proved. The difficulty of such an enterprise will not escape anyone. Finally, it should not be forgotten that by virtue of canon 6 §2 and taking account of canon 855 of the 1917 Code which is cited as the authentic source of canon 915 of the present Code, the minister will give communion if he cannot refuse the public demand of the faithful without scandal. *Mutatis mutandis*, these considerations apply to the interpretation of the prohibition which is similarly addressed to the minister against giving unction of the sick 'to those who obstinately persist in manifest grave sin' (c. 1007). Equally, one would have reasons for doubting whether the denial of ecclesiastical funeral rites provided for in the case of 'manifest sinners' applies *generally* to divorced persons who have remarried in a civil ceremony, on the one hand, and whether, on the other, every case of divorced remarried persons falls under canon 1184 §1.3°.

## Conclusion

Of all the problematical situations from a canonical point of view relating to Catholic identity, only Catholics who have become apostates, heretics and schismatics and those who have left the Church by a formal act must be considered as no longer taking part in *visible* communion with the Catholic Church (cf. c. 205). The other categories continue in general to live in *visible* communion even if their incorporation is *less full* and their participation in the life of the church is reduced or at least limited by the law.

One could have discussed the situation of Catholics cohabiting outside civil or canonical marriage or again of Catholics with eclectic beliefs and multiple adherences. However, the limits imposed on this article prevent us from this. In the face of the withdrawal of identity and the inevitable necrosis which it implies, it is best to confront problematical situations with the conviction that the canonical dispositions are not there to close off categories of persons, imprison them in a yoke or send them back to their past. The canonical norms are there to make out a way in the freedom of faith and the joy of conversion *ut felix sit Ecclesia peregrinans*.

*Translated by John Bowden*

## Notes

1. Y. Congar, 'Sur la transformation du sens de l'appartenance a l'Eglise', *Communio* 1, 5/1976, 43–4; A. Borras, 'Appartenance à l'Eglise, communion ecclésiale et excommunication. Réflexions d'un canoniste', *Nouvelle Revue Théologique* 110, 1988, 806–14.

2. A. Borras, 'Appartenance à l'Eglise ou itinérance ecclesiale?', *Lumen Vitae* 48, 1993, 161–73.

3. Cf. in the Decree of Gratian: *'De manifestis quidem loquimur: secretorum autem, et cognitor Deus, et iudex est'* (D. 32, c. 11. Cf. also X, 5, 3, 33; *DS* 1814, 2266, 2267, 3318).

4. Cf. *DS* 1201, 1203, 1205–6, 1221, 1554, 1578, 2408, 2463, 2472–8, 2615 and 3802–3; *LG* 8c.

5. Canon 916 contains a twofold exception. When there is a grave reason or no occasion to confess, one *can* receive communion, but with the obligation of an act of perfect contrition which includes the firm resolve to confess as soon as possible. In the principle that it formulates, as in the exception that it contains, c. 916 is a canonical determination of a prior dogmatic principle, namely the necessity of the state of grace for communion. It is sacramental confession that restores the state of grace, at least as a general rule, since given the impossibility of realizing it, c. 916 specifies that the act of perfect contrition is enough.

6. According to c. 1399, the penalty is facultative and indeterminate (*potest iusta poena puniri*). Consequently, this indeterminate penalty cannot be translated, according to c. 1349, either by a perpetual penalty or by a censure or remedial penalty (cc. 1331–133) except where the gravity of the case calls for a censure. In fact the application of c. 1399 is reduced to very rare instances. So in my view there is nothing to increase the singularity of the canonical notion of the delict in c. 1399. See also my critical commentary, *Les sanctions dans l'Eglise*, Paris 1990, 23–5.

7. For a critical analysis see ibid., 159–66.

8. Cf. T. Lenherr, 'Der Abfall von der katholischen Kirche durch einen formalen Akt. Versuch einer Interpretation', *Archiv für Katholisches Kirchenrecht* 152, 1983, 107–25.

# II · Institutional Dimension

# Who Speaks in the Church's Name in the Media?

## Ernest Henau

Unilateral though the definition of the Catholic Church enunciated in the seventeenth century by Bellarmine and constantly repeated since may be, it does contain several elements which have always been considered characteristics of this religious society: its massive visibility and its heavily structured hierarchical organization.[1] In fact, more than any other church, the Catholic Church can be seen in our social life, and more than any other church it has institutional points of reference. However, many things have changed in the course of the last thirty years: at least theoretically (at the level of documents) a new form of self-definition is being expressed in the Church, which, while not opposed to the elements brought out by Bellarmine, does have other accents. The Council and post-conciliar theology have attempted, in fact, to describe the Church not only as a *societas inaequalium*, i.e. a pyramidal structure with a hierarchical articulation, but also as a society of persons who are fundamentally equal in their functional diversity; not so much as a bureaucratic organization directed by a central organism, but as a 'communion' of local churches; not as an immovable bastion but as a sacrament and sign of God's salvation, which is in tension between creation (*Lumen gentium* 2) and fulfilment (*Lumen gentium* 48); not as a powerful institution but as a weak witness to the gospel in the modern world, etc. Are these changes also visible in the image that the media present of the Church? The answer to this question depends on the answer given to another question: who speaks in the name of the Catholic Church in the media? Or, to put it in another way: to whom do the media go when they want to put questions to the Catholic Church or give it space to make a statement?

In the first part of this article I want to say something about the way in which the Church is present in the media. Then I shall indicate how the media give space above all to the representatives of the hierarchy and those who challenge it. Finally, I want to examine more closely the consequences of this approach, and add some concluding comments.

Before answering the question about who speaks in the name of the Church in the media, we ought to make a distinction between different forms in which the Church is present in the media. This approach gives us the possibility of keeping this article within the limits which space imposes on it. 1. By modern media I mean here the electronic media (but what must be said about them also applies, *mutatis mutandis*, to the others, namely the written media); 2. I shall not be talking here about means of communication which the Church itself owns or about the image that the Church presents of itself in the space it buys on commercial programmes. Beginning from my experience, I shall limit myself here to public transmissions. Here the Church is presented in two ways: 1. by the allocation of a certain time to broadcasts which is structurally guaranteed and in which broadcasts are made by the religious company itself (or under the supervision of the ecclesiastical authority); 2. as the object of fortuitous information in the framework of factual programmes, like historical facts in cultural broadcasts, and quite often as the object of gentle humour or irony, biting or sarcastic mockery in entertainment programmes.

In almost all countries (at least in Europe), on the public channels (and also as an exception on commercial channels), a fixed amount of broadcasting time is assigned by the authority to the churches into which religious programmes can be inserted. This allocation is legally regulated by the legislature, and through agreements of all kinds between the broadcasting stations and the religious authority or its representatives. One can point to several models here. There is the model of the 'religious' department, which is an integral part of the (public) chain, in which the department itself is responsible for the content of the programmes. Then there are countries in which broadcasting time and the means of broadcasting are assigned to the churches and other associations on an ideological basis: these may or may not hand them over to other producers. Finally, there are countries in which the major religious currents and other ideological movements are given the possibility by the authority of creating their own small broadcasting organism which then receives broadcasting time and facilities within the framework of public broadcasting. Of course there can also be combinations of these typical models. In some countries, for example, there are so-called editorial programmes in public broadcasting; they are made by the editorial department of this organism. There are also broadcast sermons which are given under the authority of the churches.[2]

The image of the Catholic Church which appears in these broadcasts is relatively subtle. In broad outline it reflects the idea that the Church has of itself, as this has developed since Vatican II. Here not only bishops but also priests and laity speak in the name of the Church, so the community of faith does not identify itself with its hierarchical superstructure. It also appears as a local reality, and less as a highly organized religious multinational with numerous branches. Furthermore, the Church is not just represented as an ethical authority. These broadcasts also present the ecclesial community as a sacrament and sign of salvation, as a weak witness to the gospel, as a pilgrim community on the way to the fullness of its realization. Most often themes are reflected on and developed with a real sense of the necessary nuances. The essentials are distinguished from the incidentals, and so on. But the problem is that the broadcasts produced in this framework do not determine the image of the Church in public opinion. The reason for this is very simple: they are heard or viewed only by a tiny fraction of the public (including the believing public). They can only present the nuanced image of Vatican II by ignoring measures which govern the media and which according to some critics like Postman, Biser and Finkielkraut, get in the way of in-depth treatment of any serious subjects. In any case there is a kind of incompatibility between a thoughtful approach and high ratings: this creates a pressure to which the public channels are more and more exposed because of their increasing commercialization. So the image of the Church in the media is determined by the broadcasts in which (consciously or unconsciously) there is a readiness to submit to the measures alluded to above. What are these?

## Who speaks in the name of the Church in the media?

The media operate through symbols. Information becomes interesting only when it is symbolized by a concrete figure. One study has shown that the media raised the question of liberation theology above all in terms of the conflict between certain of its representatives and ecclesiastical authority, in other words, where it has symbolic figures, for example Leonardo Boff.[3] His difficulties with the Congregation for the Doctrine of Faith, personified by Cardinal Ratzinger, have the character of being an 'event', which is indispensable for the media. The study also indicates that the content of liberation theology is the object of attention only to the degree that it gives rise to conflicts. This empirical study has noted that two thirds of all the quotations from authors came from Boff, Ratzinger and the Pope.

Symbolic figures can also be necessary for other reasons, for example because of the exceptional character of their role or rank. Every country has only one (or in special cases two or three) cardinals. Because of their exceptional status, they will always appear more often in news pro-grammes. Moreover, the media prefer as a spokesperson someone with a high status. Hence priority is given to the cardinals, then to the bishops, and then to the priests. These are considered to speak more in the name of all Catholics than, for example, are the laity. Among bishops and cardinals, some stand out by reason of their strong personalities. The logic of the media leads them to value the most representative statement; it follows that the most charismatic prelate, the one who from the point of view of the media speaks in the name of the whole institution, will be given space. By virtue of the first rule I mentioned, we can note that in almost all countries, a few symbolic figures speak in the name of the whole church, often the president and to a lesser degree the spokesmen or the press chief of the episcopal conference; one or more bishops who are interesting from a media point of view.[4]

Another rule is closely connected with the previous one. The media are led to fix their attention on the sensational, whatever differs from the general norm. The preference indicated above for any kind of conflict follows this same rule. If the media give space to those who in their view hold power, then according to the rules formulated above, they also give preference to those who challenge this real or imaginary power. In this way some controversial minority groups or figures take on a significance and weight that they do not in fact have. Here the media create figures who derive their legitimacy solely from, for example, being the representatives of a particular group within the ecclesial community or making news-worthy remarks. They derive their legitimacy from the media themselves, which make them spokespersons because they correspond to a certain rule which governs these media.

As I have already noted with reference to the study on liberation theology, there is no scale of values in the media for the evaluation of items of information. That is because as a result of excessive personalization there is more interest in the event and especially its sensational, conflictual and sentimental aspects. Another factor is the speed with which above all the electronic media operate. In television the treatment of a subject is often of very limited duration. Because the media are topical, and above all because the treatment of a subject can only be very brief, a thoughtful approach is for the most part impossible, and this makes manipulation easy; besides, such a tendency is inherent in a brief and unnuanced communication. The preference of programme makers is for peripheral aspects, leaving essential elements under-exposed. Besides, it is not the style of the media to present all the subtle legal and dogmatic distinctions possible.

In addition, the journalists who present news about the Church are ordinarily uninterested in the very essence of the Church and what characterizes this essence. Because they themselves are often non-believers, they cannot of course consider the Church from the perspective of a believer. Similarly, they have little affinity for it and in some cases even an inability to familiarize themselves with the way in which believers see their faith in the Church and externalize it. This leads unbelievers to understand the church in an analogous way. This happens through the use of systems and categories which non-believers also use to assess political situations and behaviour. For it goes without saying that they want to translate standpoints of those who represent authority in the Church (according to the media) and reactions to them in terms of government and opposition, or left and right. Journalists have only a political grid on which to interpret the standpoints of the Church, and they also necessarily adopt a reductionist approach. For they only deal with subjects which in their view are of universal interest, for example anything to do with sexuality. Only a few passages are remembered of the highly developed allocutions of the Pope, and these are often only very marginal to the whole. Furthermore, the principles which the church authorities are led to put out tend to be confused with prohibitive measures. Then the argument ceases to be spiritual and becomes moral.

## Consequences for the Church

When we compare this actual situation with the self-understanding of the Church as this emerges from documents, including those of canon law, we must conclude that this situation is not an absolute reflection of the Church's judgment of itself. For example, the authority of the president of the episcopal conference is only a moral authority. Every bishop is autonomous in his own diocese, and the president of the episcopal conference has no possibility of interfering in the internal affairs of another diocese. Similarly, strictly speaking the spokesman or the press chief of the ecclesiastical province has no power. Nor does an individual bishop have any predominance over his colleagues. However, the media give the impression that some of them have only to command. Hence there is confusion among the public, which thinks that these figures are the real authorities in the church, because they apparently speak in its name. The perception of authority in the institutional church is necessarily distorted by this. Legally, all bishops are on an equal footing. But the virtual monopoly some of them have in the media creates a *de facto* inequality. One always sees the same bishops, who as a result acquire notoriety and a moral authority. So the real egalitarian structure is disturbed because the media, on the basis of their criteria, in fact give the impression that the Church is an oligarchy.[5]

This results in a paradoxical situation. In a period in the past when the Church saw itself in a much more pronounced way than in the present as being an institution with a hierarchical articulation, built in the form of a pyramid, it was looked on in this light much less than it is now. Until the electronic media became so universal, the Pope, for example, was an almost mythical figure of whom only a few men (at least outside central Italy) could form an idea from personal contact or rare representations. Only in exceptional circumstances did they learn anything about the Pope, and even then this was only little by little. At present, by means of tens of millions of television sets, the Pope penetrates everyone's living room. The hierarchy (above all the Pope) is much more visible than before.

It also follows from the way in which the media give coverage above all to the hierarchy and those who challenge it that a certain number of negative elements, essential aspects of which have led to the new understanding that the Church has acquired of itself, are hidden. Usually the Church is not considered to be a 'sign of', a sacrament which itself relates to something else. Nor is it considered an instrument instituted for the salvation of the world. It is shown principally as a battlefield of influences and powers on which, as in all institutions, there are rival interests and intrigues, conflicts and tensions. The fact that by its nature the Church is at the service of the world, as has been brought out by the conciliar documents, is never or very rarely envisaged. By explaining the Church through political categories, people come to regard it in reality much more in terms of power than in terms of service.

This reductionist approach to the Church also has an influence at another level. By giving coverage to the church authorities above all on moral matters, the media portray the Church purely and simply as an ethical authority. Furthermore, the problems are almost only those relating to the personal sphere, in connection with which the Magisterium with its demands clashes with the current social norms. Because the bishops, following the logic of the media, allow themselves to get pinned down on prohibitions, the spiritual or even pastoral dimension is almost never taken into account. In this way the Church is seen not only as an ethical authority, but above all as a repressive system. This is all the more the case since certain media presenters deliberately seek to create or reinforce this impression, albeit in a subtle way.

Because coverage is given above all to certain particular figures, as a result of a logic peculiar to the media, the local church becomes a shadow of itself. Vatican II, following New Testament and more specifically Pauline ecclesiology, stated that the Church realizes itself fully on the local level, that it becomes visible integrally in the local believing community. When symbolic figures in the sense described above appear on television or speak on the radio, the leaders of the local Christian community disappear. That is further facilitated by the fact that often there are no real media which cover the different levels of church organization. Following the same logic, the local media are equally led to turn to the same spokesmen as those at the national level: these are known, and, doubtless without wanting it, have the status of stars.

One could also illustrate the local church's loss of prestige in another way. There is a consensus among theologians that *diakonia* should be considered an essential function of the believing community (alongside the kerygma and the liturgy). And this task takes on importance because of the involvement of certain people in the framework of these activities. But here again the question of the intervention of symbolic figures arises. What the media allow to be seen of Christian *diakonia* is the action of figures known at a national or international level and not the unobtrusive commitment of members of groups which are active at the local level.

### Concluding comments

One frequent reason why in many cases the bishops above all are always forced to speak in the name of the Church is the silence, some would say even the timidity, of the laity, more particularly of Catholic intellectuals. However, since Vatican II a large number of the laity have become aware that they share the responsibility in the Church. If they are silent, the bishops feel obliged to speak. This pressure is all the stronger since, as we have seen, the logic of the media forces the bishops into the role of being the real spokesmen of the Church.

That the consequences of this situation are underestimated also emerges from the fact that there is a past history of the relationship between the media and the Church. In the past, the Church has always had an ambivalent attitude to the media. Hardly had the book been invented than the Church fought against its influence by the establishment of the Index. On the other hand it immediately made use of the book to spread 'sound doctrine'. In fact it saw that preaching in the flesh could as it were be extended in books. Its attitude to the new media (above all the electronic media) was equally reserved at the beginning, indeed negative. As in many other spheres, so too in the history of the relationship beween the Church and the media, Vatican II was a turning point. After the 1963 decree *Inter mirifica* and above all the instruction *Communio et Progressio* (1971), the Church's attitude has been much more positive. According to some commentators, the possibilities of the media (above all in this last document) have even been overestimated and idealized. We find a more realistic approach in *Aetatis novae* (1992). This document is equally concerned with a pastoral plan of social communication to be drawn up by each episcopal conference and each diocese. The way towards a plan of this kind and its contents are described in great detail. However, too little attention is paid to the way in which the image of the Church is formed in the media. On the basis of the ideas expressed here, I would want to plead for a realistic approach to the risks that the Church runs in mass communication and the dangers the media present. A new approach should go beyond the former rejection and later idealization. What is important here is a critical theory which raises the question: to what degree is it possible for the Church to subject itself to the constraints of the media, in relationship not only to the law on capital, but also to the other laws mentioned here?[6] The central question of this reflection is, who speaks in the name of the Church in the media? Unless such reflection takes place, there is a considerable chance that the image of the Church that is given will be distorted.

*Translated by John Bowden*

## Notes

1. '(The Church is) the assembly of persons who are united by the profession of the same Christian faith and communion in the same sacraments under the authority of legitimate pastors, principally by a sole representative of Christ on earth' (*Disputationes de controversiis Christianae fidei adversus hujus temporis haereticos*, II, Milan 1721, 100). Further: 'To be part of the true church at an equivalent level . . . in our view no inner virtue is required, but only the external profession of the faith and communion in the sacraments, things that are accessible to our senses. In fact the Church is an assembly as visible and as tangible as the Senate of the Roman people, the kingdom of France and the Republic of Venice' (ibid., 102).

2. Cf. E. Lever (ed.), *I Programmi religiosi alla Radio e in Televisione. Rassegna di esperienze e prospettive in Italia e in Europa*, Turin 1991.

3. Cf. M. Bleinstein, 'The Church in the Process of Social Communication. The

Conflict over the Theology of Liberation in the German Press', *Journal of Empirical Theology* 2, 1988, 51–63.

4. Cf F.-H. de Virieu, *La médiacratie*, Paris 1990, 124–52.

5. Ibid., 134.

6. Cf. O. Fuchs, *Kirche – Kabel – Kapital. Standpunkte einer christlichen Medienpolitik*, Münster 1989.

# Caritas and the Welfare State.
# The Conflict over Catholic Diakonia

## Norbert Mette

### I. Key images of Caritas – a topical discussion in Europe

What constitutes the corporate identity of church charitable work or diakonia? At the moment this question is at the top of the agenda of the Caritas organizations in Europe. There are various reasons for this. In Central and Eastern European countries which until 1989 belonged to the Warsaw Pact, it was possible for Caritas to begin organized work only after they had (re)gained their autonomy. Here the (Catholic) Church faces the problem of what plan and what structures should be envisaged for such work – though here such longer term theoretical considerations must often of course quite understandably be postponed because of the urgent need for immediate aid to a population suffering as a result of wars and catastrophes.[1] By comparison, the charitable organizations in Western European countries find themselves faced with the challenge of making an appropriate response to the advancing progress of European union. What are the tasks of the church(es), and how can or must they be perceived? That is the question, and it becomes a particularly urgent one in view of the fact that the predominance of economic policy has completely left behind the question of how joint social and political frameworks can be laid down and safeguarded in a united Europe of the future. With a few exceptions, the Caritas organizations in the countries concerned are only gradually becoming aware of this new challenge. And they find it difficult to give a joint answer, not least because the work of Caritas is conceived of and structured differently in different countries.[2] Moreover, because of the ongoing economic recession and the withdrawal of the state from its responsibility for social policy by different governments who are increasingly heedlessly pursuing the course of a neo-liberal economy, the social problems are becoming more acute in individual countries to such a degree that the 'local' charities already have more than enough to do.

All this means that the questions whether the Church must not set priorities in its charitable work or diakonia and if so, what criteria are to be applied, are becoming increasingly unavoidable. But at the same time it is also becoming clear that such a standpoint and definition of the churches' concern with welfare cannot be adopted in the abstract, but must be rooted in particular social and ecclesial conditions. This makes it worth while to consider a specific case study, namely an examination of how attempts are being made to define the identity of Caritas within the German Caritas Association. As this debate has been particularly intensive and controversial for some time, this is an obvious example to use to demonstrate the problems which arise and the various answers that can be given to them, along with their causes and consequences.

## II.  Case study: The debate about profile in the German Caritas Association

### 1.  The context of (church) welfare in Germany

The German Caritas Association, based in Freiburg im Breisgau, is an umbrella organization formed by the Caritas associations in individual dioceses and nineteen professional associations working throughout the country. In civil law it is 'a registered association . . . in canon law a "private lay association which is not a person in church law", and from the perspective of the state church part of the Catholic Church'.[3] The diocesan and professional associations are largely autonomous, and the majority of them are also legally independent. Here they are further sub-divided in a variety of ways down to the level of particular basic units (institutional organizations like hospitals, kindergartens or advisory centres, or Caritas committees in the parishes) which have specific responsibilities for everyday welfare activities. As well as a multitude of unpaid volunteer workers, in 1990 more than 350,000 paid members were in its employment. All in all about 30,000 institutions belong to the German Caritas Association in the stationary, semi-stationary and ambulant sectors, with more than a million places. The size of the clientele calling on Caritas in the course of a year amounts to several times this.

Five other leading organizations or umbrella organizations are active in Germany in the area of 'free welfare', including the parallel organization of the Protestant Church, Diakonisches Werk.[4] However, with the amount of personal resources and institutions it has to offer, Caritas holds far and away the leading place.

How that has come about is the result of a variety of factors: first, the German Caritas Association is now almost a century old (it was founded in 1897), and regional movements or the numerous charitable enterprises set up in particular by newly founded Catholic orders or communities can be dated back even earlier into the nineteenth century. So right from the beginning of their organization in Germany there have been a variety of initiatives and institutions for charitable work; and in the course of time these have been yet further developed. Secondly, the broad commitment of the churches in the sphere of welfare which is to be found today has been essentially made possible and encouraged by the fact that the legal regulation of this sphere in Germany – not least under the influence of the Catholic Church – has been undertaken in accordance with the principle of 'subsidiarity'. That means that the state has transferred a large part of welfare (guaranteed by law and largely also given public finance) to voluntary bodies which have emerged as organizations from the various ideological traditions or social and moral spheres and which in the past have beyond question helped towards the creation and development of the welfare state in Germany.

*2. Opportunities and problems in the link between the work of Caritas and the welfare state*
The close connection between church auxiliary services and the welfare state which follows from the legal regulation of welfare is something of a German peculiarity. It gives rise to a reciprocal relationship between the Church (or churches) or Caritas/Diakonia and the state, which brings both opportunities and problems. On the one hand the presuppositions for charitable or diaconal action in the church(es) are to a large degree laid down in advance by the state, with consequent financial, administrative and other dependencies. On the other hand the churches share responsibility for the welfare state and the form that it takes; moreover they have the possibility of giving a particular profile to the welfare work which they undertake, in keeping with their spiritual foundations. It is specifically over this question of profile that a controversy has recently been sparked off. If we are to be able to follow it, first of all some further comments are needed on the consequences for both sides of the interweaving of Caritas and the welfare state:

– For the church(es) this interweaving means that – not least thanks to the financial support and legal guarantee provided by the state – they can engage in diaconal work to a degree which is unique both historically and in comparison to other countries. J. Degen has made an apt assessment of this: 'With respect to diakonia, the welfare state makes a major contribution towards enabling the Church to be the Church',[5] to the extent that this is one of its basic functions.

– Conversely, bound up with this is an increase in the institutionaliza-tion of Caritas as an independent sphere of church action which encourages and establishes a tendency towards a structural separation of church aid from pastoral work with its parochial organization, and thus to a differentiation (separation) of diakonia as a 'second' church structure. Pastoral work and Caritas drift apart in a way which is pernicious for both.[6]

– Because of the increasing specialization in welfare work, in their charitable institutions churches which are active in this area are required to maintain certain standards in technical equipment and the professionalism of their personnel. In addition, welfare work becomes strongly legalized and bureaucratized. Honorary 'laity' have increasing difficulty in finding a satisfying sphere of activity in Caritas.

– Conversely, the relatively good image that the churches have with the public as 'diaconal service organizations' contributes to a considerable part of the population remaining church members, even if in other respects they do not play an active part in church life.[7]

– For the state, it is an advantage to be able to resort to the social commitment of the churches (or other voluntary welfare workers), since, first, it has no resources for motivating such help and, secondly, it is to a large degree dependent on the volatile attitude of the electorate towards social welfare policies.[8]

– At the same time, because of the subsidiarity in the involvement of the churches in the sphere of welfare, the state can count on their fundamental loyalty. In fact there are constant signs that in cases of doubt the churches are politically rationing their advocacy of the poor and the handicapped so that there is no complete break with the prevailing policy.

The aspects indicated suggest that the involvement of the churches in the welfare state in Germany has not been a problem for a long time because to a considerable degree it is in accord with the interests of both parties. Moreover, this has the advantage for Caritas or Diakonisches Werk as organizations that they occupy a relatively autonomous intermediate position between the church(es) and the state, giving them the possibility of being active in criticizing and shaping on both sides. However, there is no guarantee that this situation will last. On the contrary, there are growing signs that developments are under way which could result in deep-seated changes in the laissez-faire collaboration of church and state. Thus for example in the face of a social policy which is becoming increasingly restrictive – combined with massive social demolition which makes poverty a fact which can no longer be overlooked in a prosperous society – the churches increasingly find themselves confronted with the question how credible their prophetic function as advocates for those affected can be if they are unwilling to drop their loyalty to the government which is responsible for this anti-social policy.

A further point is that because of legal provisions in welfare work, the possibility of giving an independent profile, say, to existing institutions is getting smaller and smaller and this is increasingly being forced to the periphery; the original location of volunteers and their traditions and milieus is becoming increasingly insignificant for the concrete organization of welfare. In addition, further changes are taking place within diakonia or Caritas itself, like the fact that the orders or communities which for decades have been involved in maintaining welfare institutions and supporting them are facing recruitment problems. This is the complex background against which the current discussion of image is being carried on within the German Caritas Association.

## 3. *In search of an identity for Caritas in a (developed) welfare state*

This search is far from easy, simply because in the course of time Caritas has taken on such different areas. Furthermore, there are fundamentally different theological views about defining the identity of Caritas:

– One position, which has been put forward particularly strikingly by H. Pompey,[9] begins by noting that the process of dissociation from the Church which can be seen throughout society can also be seen in the charitable sphere, in so far as a considerable number of those involved here have distanced themselves from the Church, with the result that it is increasingly difficult to identify the specific character of Caritas – in contrast to the time when it was still strongly stamped by the involvement of members of orders. What is therefore needed is reflection on the 'association philosophy' of Caritas, which Pompey thinks can be derived from theology through some relevant christological, anthropological and ecclesiological arguments. The result is that he defines Caritas as a fundamental realization of church community and sees the hierarchy as ultimately responsible for the concrete form which it takes. Involvement in charitable institutions is to be made dependent on a readiness to enter into a binding commitment to the criteria thus arrived at; these criteria are to be fixed as legal conditions of employment and to be met by voluntary conviction, which is to be encouraged by an appropriate spiritual supervision which will help to provide a deeper foundation for the professional competence of those concerned. If it is no longer possible to hold on to existing personnel on these conditions, the Church must leave the sphere of charitable action and see that this is handed over to 'general social welfare organizations' which could be conceived of independently of church tasks. The Church could then press on with giving profile to the few institutions left to it in accordance with its mission.

– If the concern of this position is to direct and guarantee the identity of Caritas, particularly through the selection of personnel by means of particular criteria of church allegiance and by contracts of employment, the other position – which is represented especially by R. Zerfass[10] – objects that this would inevitably result in a legalism which did not correspond to the gospel. What gives charitable work its ecclesial – or better, Christian – character is an intrinsic quality which makes it credible, and is to be demonstrated in the institutions shaped by it; it cannot be ordained once and for all by particular authorities. The search for the identity of Caritas should have the form of a process in which all concerned take part. 'This is work towards the shared vision of Christians who, whether in paid work or in an honorary capacity, have resolved to seek to meet the needs of their fellow human beings, together and with all men and women of good will. The need is to develop criteria of an ecclesial nature which restore to Caritas its character of invitation and evangelization, by understanding it as a sphere in which one can discover the gospel together with others – not as an area signposted by the Church into which only full-blooded Catholics can be admitted.'[11] Thus the definition of the identity of Caritas becomes a quest for a common vision which can be made concrete in different ways depending on context and tradition. Moreover, where diakonia is performed in such a way that it can be experienced as the testimony of Jesus Christ, the Church already becomes event and is a challenge to the rest of the Church to be converted by the gospel.

In contrast to the position which was sketched out first, it is striking that this second position adopts a more complex course in its search for the identity of Caritas: it does not just define – in terms of organizational sociology – the 'personnel' as variables, while the programme and the organization remain unchangeable tasks, as does the first position; rather, it brings these different aspects of organized Caritas together in a dynamic relationship and in addition introduces the historical dimension. Moreover, theologically it operates with categories (like God's universal will to salvation, discipleship of Jesus, the Church as the people of God) which for their part support a dynamic understanding of identity; here the issue is the identification of characteristics which can be cited as typical of welfare with a Christian inspiration, without wanting to make an exclusive claim for it.[12] In terms of church law, at first sight it seems simpler to define the identity of Caritas in accordance with the first position, since for it the responsible subject is clearly the hierarchical ministry. However, the second position can appeal to the church's law of association, which allows free associations of believers, as the Caritas associations originally were, and by so doing assigns the 'authority of the charism' its appropriate sphere of perceiving its responsibility – in supplementing and correcting the institutional ministry.[13]

However, what is characteristic of both positions is that they make their particular definition of the identity of Caritas from a theological, internal church perspective, even though in each case the accents are different. In view of the traditional neglect of this field of church action in theology and pastoralia, this certainly represents an important correction. Nevertheless we must ask whether it does not neglect the social status of church diakonia. What stands in the foreground is the question of the credibility of the action; the problem of which specific possibilities can be and are to be identified by charitable church action under the conditions of the specific form of socialization in the welfare state remains a secondary one.

Precisely this is the starting point for the five options of the work of the Caritas association which K. Gabriel has offered for discussion; with their different emphases they aim at reminding the welfare state that has developed critically of its origin in the Christian tradition and of the legacy it continues to preserve.[14] In detail, these are the options:

– for a 'culture of participation' which aims at the participation and responsibility of all in solidarity, and thus is opposed to the exclusion above all of the weak in society;

– for a policy advocating the participation in the life of society of all those who are concerned to eliminate poverty from society;

– for mediation between formal and informal systems of help which counter the increasing attachment of care to the 'logic of the system' and the colonization of life that goes with it;

– for the encouragement and development of community diakonia in subsidiarity in a way which is orientated on the neighbourhood and is thus in principle particularly sensitive to new needs, but which is threatened with a take-over by the welfare organizations which work on a large scale;

– and for the opening up of well-to-do German society to its worldwide social responsibility, clearly repudiating the increased selfishness of the nationalistic welfare state.

So according to Gabriel's view the particular involvement of the church(es) in public welfare which has become characteristic of Germany offers the possibility and at the same time the obligation to become the advocate(s) of the welfare state and emphatically to oppose all efforts to undermine it. In this way the sharp dividing line between the 'organizational approach' and the 'animation approach' to charitable work which is often drawn in the international comparison of different profiles of organized Caritas will be blurred.[15] For in that case the maintaining of one's own institutions would in no way be a fundamental obstacle to Caritas, but rather would offer it a specific chance not only as a Samaritan to care for the victims of robbery but also to demonstrate the structural causes of robbery and take action against them.[16] In reality, however, it is proving increasingly difficult to take this chance, especially when it might cause danger to existing institutions. Only in the disputed case of abortion has the Catholic Church in Germany so far given the example of making itself independent of state influences (for instance over financing advisory centres), in order to be able to put forward its own position consistently in public and thus impose itself as much as possible.

It is impossible to forecast what future the traditional welfare system in Germany, organized along the lines of subsidiarity, will have. As I have indicated, some more or less deep-seated changes are under way. In addition to the restrictions to which the welfare associations are at present exposed to because of the changes (legal, financial etc.) in, if not the reconstruction of, the welfare state, it is experiencing increased competition from free service organizations which organize their aid by market criteria and are (can be) particularly in demand among those who can afford the considerable financial expense. In this sphere, too, there is clearly a tendency towards a social segregation which is advancing with increasing tenacity; this is intensified by the pressure towards individualization which is making 'solidarity' increasingly an alien word in social vocabulary.

The German Caritas Association in particular, like Diakonisches Werk, is being asked more and more persistently what interests its institutions serve or seek to serve. There is something to be said for the argument that sooner or later the churches will not be able to avoid deciding whether with their Caritas or Diakonia they want to go on acting as intermediaries between the welfare state and its clientele in need of help, or whether – choosing the 'option for the poor and the others' – in a partisan way they take the side of those who are increasingly being forced to the edge of society or even right outside it. At all events, the challenges to the churches to object to and fight against state measures for mercy's sake may be more rather than less.

*Translated by John Bowden*

## Notes

1. Cf. the informative articles on the situation and development of Caritas in some Eastern European countries in Deutscher Caritasverband (ed.), *caritas '94. Jahrbuch des Deutschen Caritasverbandes*, Freiburg 1993, 52–65.

2. Cf. E. Gillen, 'Caritas-Leitbilder in Europa', *caritas '94*, 1993, 304–14, and the other articles in this issue.

3. M. N. Ebertz, 'Caritas im gesellschaftlichen Wandel – Expansion in die Kirche?', in M. Lehner and W. Zauner (eds.), *Grundkurs Caritas*, Linz 1993, 83–114: 91; cf. for what follows also ibid., 86–92.

4. See J. Degen, 'Diakonia as an Agency in the Welfare State', *Concilium* 24, 1988, 102–109, esp. 102f.

5. Ibid., 106.

6. Cf. H. Steinkamp, 'Diakonia in the Church of the Rich and the Church of the Poor', ibid., 65–75: 65f.

7. Cf. K. Gabriel, 'Optionen verbandlicher Caritas im Wandel der sozialstaatlich organisierten Gesellschaft', *caritas '93*, Freiburg 1992, 250–8: 253.

8. Cf. ibid., 254.

9. Cf. H. Pompey, 'Das Profil der Caritas und die Identität ihre Mitarbeiter/innen', *caritas '93*, 11–26; id., 'Entlastung für die Mitarbeiter', *Herderkorrespondenz* 47, 1993, 317–19.

10. Cf. R. Zerfass, 'Das Proprium der Caritas als Herausforderung an die Träger', *caritas '93* (n. 9), 27–40; id., *Lebensnerv Caritas*, Freiburg 1992.

11. Zerfass, 'Proprium' (n. 10), 29.

12. Cf. Gillen, 'Leitbilder' (n. 2), 310.

13. Cf. here in more detail W. Fürst, 'Pastorale Diakonie – Diakonische Pastoral', in N. Feldhoff and A. Dünner (ed.), *Die verbandliche Caritas*, Freiburg 1991, 52–80: 70–2.

14. Cf. Gabriel, 'Optionen' (n. 7), 255ff.

15. Cf. Gillen, 'Leitbilder' (n. 2), 304f., 308f.

16. See Bishop Franz Kamphaus's letter to those working in charitable welfare institutions in the diocese of Limburg, dated 24 February 1993, 2.

# Catholic Hospitals: How Catholic Will They Be?

## John P. Beal

The Catholic Church has a long history of incarnating its concern for the sick and dying in health care institutions. In 1990, there were 5,946 acute-care facilities, 14,300 dispensaries, 732 leprosaria, and 11,018 long-term care facilities operating under Catholic auspices throughout the world.[1] Although sponsorship arrangements vary from country to country, institutionalized health care under Catholic auspices gives the Church a visible presence in societies throughout the world. Forces both external and internal to the Church shape the climate in which Catholic health care facilities operate and challenge their Catholic identity. Although this article deals primarily with Catholic health care in the United States, health care institutions in other countries face similar problems.

### I. Forces shaping Catholic health care

*(a) External forces*
 1. Health care is increasingly treated not as a priceless form of compassionate service, but as a commodity subject to the same market forces as any other consumer good. The relationships of providers, consumers, payers and policy makers are more and more shaped by economic considerations. Since the health care system has surplus capacity, providers must compete with one another for market share. Selfless service to the sick and dying does not flourish in this competitive climate.
 2. For-profit hospitals and systems have grown rapidly in number and in market share. Survival of non-profit Catholic facilities has often dictated that they reorganize into horizontally and vertically integrated systems and

diversify their services.[2] Thus, Catholic facilities have engaged in joint ventures with other providers and spun off new for-profit subsidiaries in fields related and even unrelated to health care to provide revenue for their more traditional services. The dangers for polycorporate Catholic institutions are that decisions about what services to provide will be made on the basis not of community need but of profitability, that corporate third parties will be inserted in the relationship between patient and care-giver, and that joint ventures with non-Catholic providers will entail cooperation in activities antithetical to Catholic values.

3. The more economic considerations dominate health care delivery, the more the economically disadvantaged are squeezed out of the health care market. It is estimated that 35 million Americans are without any health care insurance while countless others have inadequate coverage.[3] Catholic hospitals were originally founded to serve the needs of the poor and were supported by philanthropy. Later, care for the poor was subsidized by shifting the costs to patients with the ability to pay (usually through third-party insurers). As government and private insurers enact cost-cutting measures, subsidizing charity care through cost-shifting is growing unfeasible. Thus, many Catholic hospitals face a dilemma: they must either maintain their commitment to the poor and face bankruptcy or maintain solvency and abandon the poor.

*(b) Internal factors*

1. Catholic health care facilities are overwhelmingly the legacy of women's religious institutes. As the number of religious women declines, it is becoming difficult for institutes to provide a visible presence in their facilities or even on their governing boards. Care-givers, supervisors, and policy-makers in Catholic hospitals are now predominantly lay people. The maintenance of Catholic identity hinges on the commitment of these lay people to Catholic values.

2. Catholic hospitals have long histories of caring for all patients regardless of creed. Even before equal opportunity employment requirements, demand for competent personnel introduced a rich pluralism to the staffs of Catholic facilities at all levels. Today, from board room to laundry room, Catholic facilities' personnel include both Catholics and non-Catholics, who see their work primarily as a job and not as a ministry. In this pluralistic atmosphere, maintaining fidelity to authentic Catholic values is an ongoing challenge.

3. Literature on Catholic health care facilities underscores their communitarian character. Although the ideal of building communities of service is inspiring, communitarian rhetoric inevitably rings hollow. It is

hard to imagine an institution more impervious to communitarian trends than contemporary hospitals. In addition to the centrifugal effect of ever greater specialization in the medical profession, hospitals are rigidly stratified institutions with little upward or downward mobility. Administrators, medical staff, nurses, technicians, housekeeping and maintenance personnel, and others all cling tightly and at times protectively to their group's place in the operation. Fostering community in such caste-riddled institutions is a baffling challenge.

## II.  Changing models in Catholic health care

### (a) From 'family business' to 'franchise'

These external and internal forces show little sign of abating. Instead, they are rapidly rendering obsolete traditional ways of defining and maintaining the Catholic identity of health care facilities. Most Catholic health care facilities were founded as free-standing institutional apostolates of religious institutes. Although local ordinaries approved their establishment and retained visitation and oversight rights,[4] they functioned as 'family businesses' of the founding religious institutes. The institutes owned, operated, and in large measure staffed their health care facilities. Immersed in the charism of their institutes through religious formation, members of these religious families were present throughout their organizations and their spirit permeated these facilities.[5]

In the aftermath of Vatican II, changes in the Church and the health care system radically altered these 'family businesses'. Catholic health care institutions began an irreversible shift from a 'family business' model to a 'franchise' model.[6] Free-standing facilities gave way to multi-corporate holding companies and eventually co-ordinated or integrated health care delivery systems. Declining involvement by religious in health care ministry, underdeveloped ministry formation programmes for lay participants in health care, and rapid increases in the size and complexity of health care facilities overwhelmed traditional systems for communicating and maintaining Catholicity.

### (b) Introduction of the civil-law corporation

An early omen of the shift of Catholic health care facilities from 'family businesses' to 'franchises' was the move to establish institutional apostolates as civil-law corporations distinct from sponsoring religious institutes. The aim of separate incorporation was to shield religious institutes from liability for activities of their health care institutions and to enhance these institutions' eligibility for public funds. While religious institutes continued to sponsor these facilities and usually retained some measure of control over them, responsibility for day-to-day operations was vested in boards of trustees composed of lay people and some religious. The effect of separate incorporation of health care facilities on the canonical status of their property became a hotly disputed issue among canonists.

John McGrath claimed that separate incorporation conveys ownership of a facility's assets from the sponsoring religious institute to the new civil law corporation.[7] Thus, this property is no longer subject to canonical norms on administration and alienation of church property. Adam Maida countered that civil incorporation effects no change in the canonical status of the property of a Catholic health care facility. Consequently, administration and alienation of these assets must comply with canonical norms.[8] In fact, the canonical status of the property of Catholic health care facilities is a vastly more complex issue than the theses of McGrath and Maida claim and must be determined by case by case analyses.[9]

The canonical status of the property of Catholic health care facilities is not an insignificant issue. However, the dominance of canonical discussions of Catholic health care facilities in the United States by the McGrath-Maida debate has created the comforting but erroneous impression that the Catholic identity of a health care facility is established and guaranteed solely by the ownership and control of its property by an ecclesiastical public juridic person. A similar myopia has affected the canonical discussion in Germany, where concern to preserve the autonomy of Catholic charitable institutions from state control has led to an almost exclusive focus on the juridic relationship of these facilities to hierarchical authority.[10] Fixation on the juridic status of an institution or its property has allowed canonical discussions of Catholic identity to proceed without sufficient advertence to the rapidly changing climate within which these facilities operate and with little reference to factors internal to health care facilities that decisively shape their Catholic identity.

To define and foster Catholic identity of health care institutions as they are transmuted from 'family businesses' to 'franchises' requires vision and courage. On the one hand, the Catholic identity of facilities needs to be defined in a way that is both theologically adequate and in conformity with their present configuration. On the other hand, equal or greater attention must be given to internal policies, practices, and corporate cultures which translate Catholic identity from rhetoric to reality.

## III. Defining a Catholic health care facility

### (a) Catholic health care in the Church

Catholic health care facilities do not exist 'in the world' with merely extrinsic links to the Church. They live and move and have their being *in* the Church, 'the whole vast body of people that once arose out of the event of Christ and lives still to bring him to the world for its redemption'.[11] Health care facilities participate in the Church's redemptive mission and, therefore, perform a ministry in and for the Church. This ministry is service that empowers the infirm to rise above the physical, psychological and spiritual ravages of illness and old age and to realize their human and Christian potential.[12] Thus, health care facilities exist in the Church to incarnate and realize the love of neighbour and respect for the dignity of each person that the Church preaches.

### (b) Bonds of communion

As institutions 'in the Church', health care facilities necessarily are in communion with the Church's hierarchical leadership. This communion is expressed in three essential ways: the facility's adherence to Catholic moral and ethical teaching, provision of pastoral care to patients and staff, and establishment of some canonical relationship between the facility and hierarchical leadership.

1. Conformity with Church teaching on medico-moral issues is usually achieved by incorporating episcopal directives into the facility's governing documents.[13] However, compliance with such directives alone cannot insure the Catholicity of a health care facility. Primarily devoted to proscribing procedures considered incompatible with magisterial teaching, episcopal directives usually define what Catholic facilities may not do but not what they must do and be.

2. The canonical bond between a health care facility and hierarchical authority can take a variety of forms.

(a) *The traditional sponsorship model.* The traditional and still most common form is establishment and sponsorship of a facility by a single religious institute with the approval of the diocesan bishop. Catholicity is fostered by the facility's connection with the public juridic person of the sponsoring institute and the diocesan bishop's oversight of the facility, even though the facility itself may not be a public juridic person in the Church. The circumstances of the facility's establishment and the effects of any subsequent re-structurings determine whether its assets are church property.

Many institutes have structured their health care facilities as civil-law membership corporations. By reserving to the members of the corporation (usually the canonical leadership of the sponsoring institute) critical powers over the facility, this model allows institutes to retain control over the Catholicity and direction of facilities they sponsor despite their declining numbers.

As pressures on freestanding facilities have mounted, there has been a move toward joint sponsorship of networks and systems of health care facilities by several religious institutes and consolidation of the facilities of individual institutes into large systems. As regional and multi-regional systems and networks play a greater role in health care delivery, however, consideration will have to be given to vesting responsibility for oversight of Catholic health care with the episcopal conference rather than with the diocesan bishop of the place where an individual facility of a system is located.

(b) *Alternative sponsorship models*. Given the doubt about the future capacity of religious institutes to continue effective sponsorship of health care even as corporate members, alternative sponsorship models have been proposed. In health care facilities as in other institutions, maintaining Catholic identity requires more than Catholic language in mission statements and corporate documents. A 'critical mass' of strategically located participants in the facility's ministry must be dedicated to its redemptive mission. It was religious who provided this 'critical mass' in the past; lay people alone or in concert with religious will have to provide it in the future. The critical challenge is to develop effective formation programmes for lay leaders and participants in health care ministry, perhaps through enlisting religious 'as mentors and "sponsors" of the next generation of sponsors'.[14]

The revised Code of Canon Law provides vehicles for structuring new forms of sponsorship.

(i) Where a lay or mixed group committed to continuing the mission of Catholic health care has already emerged, competent ecclesiastical authority (c. 312) can erect it as a public association of the faithful which *ipso iure* enjoys public juridic personality and carries out its mission 'in the name of the Church' (c. 313). While public associations enjoy a certain autonomy, their statutes must be approved by competent authority (c. 314), their membership is limited to Catholics in good standing (c. 316), their property administered according to the norms for church property, and their activities subject to oversight and possibly intervention by competent authority (cc. 317–319). Erecting a sponsor of a health care institution as a public association ties it tightly to the juridic structure of the Church.

Some have argued that it is only through a structure in which health care is carried out in the name of the Church by an ecclesiastical public juridic person that the ecclesial nature of charitable undertakings can be given adequate expression.[15] This position seems to be based on an impoverished ecclesiology according to which the only form of truly ecclesial activity is that conducted by canonical mission from the hierarchy. While it is true that it is the responsibility of the diocesan bishop to promote apostolic works in the diocese and to see to their proper coordination (c. 394, §1), neither the code nor the conciliar texts on which it is based require or even suggest that all organized or institutional apostolic endeavours must be seen as extensions of the bishop's own ministry. Nor is there anything in the nature of health care ministry that would make it one whose pursuit is by its nature reserved to ecclesiastical authority (c. 301, §1). Indeed, the particular combination of professional skill and Christian dedication required for health care ministry would seem to qualify it as one particularly appropriate for lay people. Thus, although a public association of the faithful is a vehicle available for the continuation of Catholic health care sponsorship, it is not the only acceptable or even the preferred model.

(ii) In virtue of baptism, the faithful share in the mission of the Church and have the right to found associations and initiate charitable works. They cannot, however, designate these undertakings as Catholic without the consent of ecclesiastical authority (cc. 216–217). Nothing prevents members of the faithful, as individuals or as groups, from establishing a health care facility in the Catholic tradition or taking over the operation of an existing facility when the sponsoring community withdraws. However, the diocesan bishop's permission is required for the faithful to designate or continue to designate their facility as 'Catholic'. While the bishop must ascertain the genuineness of the facility's Catholicity and monitor its continued compliance with Catholic principles (c. 305, §1), a 'Catholic' facility of this kind has no other institutional connection with church structures.

(iii) Should the faithful desire a more formal status within the Church for the sake of insuring the continuity of the Catholic identity of an institution, they could seek recognition as a private association of the faithful from competent authority (c. 299, §§1–3). Recognition requires review of the association's statutes by the competent authority, who can also grant the association status as a private juridic person in the Church. Membership in private associations is not limited to Catholics, but can be extended to non-Catholics dedicated to the association's ministry.[16] Although subject to the vigilance of competent authority who may suppress it if its activity deviates from Catholic doctrine or discipline (c. 326, §1), a private association enjoys legitimate autonomy in the conduct of its affairs (c. 323, §1). Even if granted private juridic personality, a private association's property is administered according to its statutes and applicable civil law (c. 325).

Some have suggested that it is desirable to grant private juridic personality to private associations engaged in institutional health care ministry because this status focuses attention on the work of the association rather than on the persons composing it. However, the Catholic identity of an institution is dependent less on its juridic status than on the dedication and spirituality of those who participate in its work. Consequently, attention should be focused on the members of the association and their formation as health care ministers (c. 329).

For nearly a century, private associations have provided a Catholic presence in health care and other charitable institutions in Germany.[17] Their private status does not seem to have weakened the Catholic identity of these institutions. Recently there have been experiments in the United States with private associations as sponsors of Catholic hospitals when the founding religious institutes were forced to withdraw. Too little data is available on these experiments to determine the effectiveness of private associations in preserving Catholic identity of health care institutions in the United States.

## IV.  Being a Catholic health care facility

Regardless of the juridic form a health care facility's relationship with hierarchical authority takes, neither civil nor canon law can guarantee its Catholic identity. Catholicity hinges critically on the commitment of its personnel to health care as a ministry. In this regard, three factors are vital: quality care, pursuit of social justice, and concern for the poor.[18]

(a)  The quality of medical care provided in Catholic facilities cannot be inferior to that provided in its non-Catholic and secular counterparts. However, a Catholic facility ministers to the whole person – body, mind and spirit. Such holistic health care requires attention not only to the scientific quality of the medical care provided but to the way in which it is provided. As the late André Hellegers observed,

> As the caring branches of medicine were gradually pushed aside by the curing ones, there seemed to be less use for the Christian virtues. I think that shortly the need for these old Christian virtues will return and once again be at a premium. Our patients will need a helping hand and not a

helping knife. This is no time to dismantle the low-technology care model of medicine.[19]

Although there is nothing uniquely Catholic in such quality care, in the popular mind it is this personal touch that distinguishes Christian facilities from secular.[20]

(b) The credibility of the Church's proclamation of the gospel is undermined when its own internal life, including that of its health care facilities, does not mirror the justice it preaches. Catholic facilities need to be attentive to the demands of social justice when they make decisions about what services to offer and how to allocate their resources. These decisions should be made in the light of the real health care needs of the communities they serve rather than of merely financial considerations. The Church's social teaching must also inform employer-employee relations in these facilities.

(c) Market pressures may prevent Catholic facilities from increasing substantially the amount of care it provides to the indigent in the near future. Nevertheless, they can respect the dignity of those poor patients they do serve by giving them the same quality of care and the same personal attention they give to the better-off. They can also advocate vigorously public policies that ensure equitable access to the health care system for the poor. Decisions about where to locate facilities, which types of services to provide or discontinue, and what sort of equipment to purchase should be made in the light of their impact on the poor.

## V. Conclusion

Catholic institutions have a long and distinguished history of service to the sick and the dying. Rapid changes in the health care system and in the church pose daunting challenges to these institutions' ability to continue to provide care in a manner that is authentically Catholic. Canon law can assist in maintaining the Catholic identities of these facilities. However, how Catholic they will be in the future depends primarily on the leadership, creative imagination and faithful commitment of those who are convinced that health care is not a job but a ministry.

## Notes

1. Secretary of State, *Annuarium Statisticum Ecclesiae*, Vatican City 1990, 329. In the same year, 644 hospitals, 148 dispensaries, 2 leprosaria and 11,018 long-term care facilities in the United States were sponsored by Catholic agencies (ibid., 323).

2. P. Starr, *The Social Transformation of American Medicine*, New York 1982, 420–49.

3. Catholic Health Association, *No Room in the Marketplace*, Saint Louis 1986, 2.

4. 1917 Code, cc. 1489, §2 and 1491, §1.

5. Consolidated Catholic Health Care, *Critical Choices: Catholic Health Care in the Midst of Transformation*, Oak Brook, IL 1993, 5–7.

6. Ibid.

7. J. McGrath, *Catholic Institutions in the United States*, Washington 1968.

8. A. Maida, *Ownership, Control and Sponsorship of Catholic Institutions*, Harrisburg 1975. More recently, A. Maida and N. Cafardi, *Church Property, Church Finances, and Church Related Corporation*, Saint Louis 1984.

9. R. Kennedy, 'McGrath, Maida, Michiels: Introduction to a Study of the Canonical and Civil-Law Status of Church-Related Institutions in the United States', *The Jurist* 50, 1990, 351–401.

10. A. Bamberg, *Hôpital et Églises*, Strasbourg 1987, 234–44.

11. J. Komonchak, 'The Catholic University in the Church', in *Catholic Universities in Church and Society*, Washington 1993, 38.

12. R. McCormick, *Health and Medicine in the Catholic Tradition*, New York 1984, 20–4.

13. The National Conference of Catholic Bishops of the United States approved such directives in November of 1971. United States Catholic Conference, *Ethical and Religious Directives for Catholic Health Care Facilities*, Washington 1971.

14. Consolidated Catholic Health Care, *Critical Choices* (n. 5), 35.

15. H. Heinemann, 'Die Rechtsstellung des Deutschen Caritasverbandes und der Diözesanverbände und ihre Einordnung in das Gesetzbuch der Kirche', *Archiv für katholisches Kirchenrecht* 158, 1989, 428. See also A. Hierold, *Grundlegung und Organisation kirchlicher Caritas unter besonderer Berücksichtigung des deutschen Teilkirchenrechtes* (MthStkan 38), St Ottilien 1979, 137. North American authors like Maida who contend that the assets of health care institutions must be those of a public juridic person if the facility is to be considered Catholic seem to hold a similar position.

16. H. Heinemann, 'Die Mitgleidschaft nichtkatholischer Christen in kirchlichen Vereinen', *Archiv für katholisches Kirchenrecht* 153, 1984, 416–26.

17. Heinemann, 'Die Rechtsstellung' (n. 15), 418–28.

18. See J. K. Deblois, *The Catholic Hospital: An Analysis and Critique*, Washington 1987, 133–63.

19. Cited in McCormick, *Health and Medicine* (n. 12), 41.

20. See Bamberg, *Hôpital* (n. 10), 270–89.

# From the University which is really Catholic to the University which is legally Catholic

## Roch Pagé

The Code of Canon Law devotes two chapters to universities. The first (cc. 807–14) discusses Catholic universities, and the second (cc. 815–21) ecclesiastical universities. If the essential elements of the latter are well defined, the same cannot be said of the former, whose very nature emerges only in comparison with that of ecclesiastical universities.[1] It has to be said that the latter already profited from the illumination in the apostolic constitution *Sapientia christiana*,[2] promulgated in 1979, four years before the Code, which was the revision of a first document devoted to ecclesiastical universities by Pope Pius XI in 1931.[3] In the case of Catholic universities, the opposite happened, with the promulgation in 1990 of the apostolic constitution *Ex corde Ecclesiae*.[4]

Before the promulgation of the Code, the Catholic universities did not have an official document to guide them over their Catholic identity. The 1917 Code was not much help here, since it was in fact dealing with ecclesiastical universities, with only a hint of the existence of Catholic universities. Nor should it be surprising that *Sapientia christiana* still considers the ecclesiastical universities to be a kind of Catholic university.[5] Does not the International Federation of Catholic Universities approved by Pope Pius XII in 1949, i.e. after *Deus scientiarum Dominus*, lump them all together?

However, the universities within the Federation did not wait for the Code to reflect on their Catholic identity. For a university established by the Holy See, the question does not arise, or at any rate does not do so in the same way as it does for those universities which were founded by private initiatives. For the most part, their statutes are the stable memory of their origin and aims, identifying the competent ecclesiastical authority and determining where it intervenes, something which is not always self-evident in other cases.

Though the question of the Catholic identity of universities was neither its occasion nor its first aim, research undertaken by the Federation on the mission of the Catholic university in the Church and the modern world nevertheless shed important light in the form of a document entitled 'The Catholic University in the Modern World'.[6] Even if this is not an official document of the Holy See, the Congregation for Catholic Education nevertheless studied it at a plenary assembly, the 'results of which have been approved by the Holy Father'.[7] As it was found 'valuable though requiring improvement', it is very important to take account of it here, since the Code, and even more *Ex corde Ecclesiae*, can be presumed to contain these improvements.

Even if chronologically 'The Catholic University in the Modern World' preceded the promulgation of the Code, the fact remains that the document contained elements which the Code did not replace because of their clarity and which could continue to guide the universities concerned. That is no longer the case after *Ex corde Ecclesiae*. That is why the Catholic identity of universities will first be studied according to the Code and then according to the document, before being considered according to the apostolic constitution itself.

## I. The Catholic identity of the university according to the Code of Canon Law

The Code does not indicate what characteristics allow a university to be called Catholic, any more than it gives a definition of a Catholic university. Canon 808 speaks of a university which is 'really Catholic' (*reapse catholica*), which is what c. 803 §3 says of the school, but without stating what this expression denotes. However, it is possible, by gleaning this and that from the chapter devoted to Catholic universities, to determine that in addition to those which bear 'the title or name Catholic university' (c. 808) this category includes those which have been established 'by the Church' or are directed by it (cf. c. 807).

It is enough to read the eight relevant canons of the Code to see that the emphasis is put on the formal or external aspect of the Catholic identity of universities. They clearly indicate that Catholic universities are those which have bonds of an indeterminate nature with a competent ecclesiastical authority and which give to the said authority rights and duties including vigilance. For example: 'the conferences of bishops are to see to it . . . '; 'it is the responsibility of the authority who is competent in accord with the statutes . . .' (801 §1); 'the conference of bishops and the diocesan bishops concerned have the duty and right . . . ' (id., §2), etc.

As for the more material or internal elements which characterize the Catholic university, they are certainly present in the legislation, but not in any systematic way. They have to be sought among the various fields in which the vigilance of the competent authority is exercised.

These material elements can only be understood in the light of the whole of the very first canon of the chapter, which lists the three aims of the Catholic university: to contribute to a higher level of human culture, to a fuller advancement of the human person, and also 'to the fulfilment of the Church's teaching office' (c. 807). It is clear that this last aim sums up the two others, of which it becomes as it were the main vehicle. This is also the aim which is pursued by the competent authority when it exercises its right or duty of vigilance with regard to the Catholic university. Thus the teaching becomes the central element of the Catholic identity of a university according to the Code.

According to c. 809, it is for conferences of bishops to see that there are universities in which various disciplines are taught with due regard to their academic autonomy, but 'with due consideration for Catholic doctrine'. Moreover, it seems to be taken for granted that in Catholic universities there will be 'a faculty of theology, an institute of theology, or at least a chair of theology so that classes may be given for lay students' (c. 811 §1). And to ensure that the bond between faith and culture or a 'fuller advancement of the human person' shall be achieved adequately, it is provided that 'in the individual Catholic universities classes should be given which treat in a special way those theological questions which are connected with the disciplines of their faculties' (id., §2).

Moreover, as for teachers in Catholic universities, 'the competent authority according to the statutes' is to see that they are 'outstanding in their integrity of doctrine and probity of life'.[8] Although there are statutes, c. 810 §2 imposes on the conferences of bishops and the bishops concerned 'the duty and right of being vigilant that in these universities the principles of Catholic doctrine are faithfully observed'. So it should not be surprising that when it comes to the teaching of theological disciplines themselves, the teachers must 'have a mandate from the competent ecclesiastical authority'.[9]

Indeed, it must be accepted that apart from universities bearing the name or the title of 'Catholic university' or those which had been established or were directed by the Church, there were few who could recognize their Catholic identity with certainty from the different fields of application of the vigilance of the 'competent ecclesiastical authority' according to the Code. It was certainly easier for most of them to describe themselves as Catholic on the basis of the document 'The Catholic University in the Modern World',[10] approved by the participants in the Second Congress of Delegates of World Catholic Universities which met at Rome in 1972.

## II. The Catholic identity of the university according to 'The Catholic University in the Modern World'

According to the final document of the Second Congress of Delegates of World Catholic Universities, it is the material or internal elements which constitute the essentials of the Catholic identity of a university. In fact the very first clause of the document, dealing with the goal of the Catholic university – 'to provide in institutional form a Christian presence in the university world in the face of the great problems of contemporary society' – sets out its four essential characteristics like this:

1. A Christian inspiration, not only individual but communal.
2. A continuing effort to reflect in the light of the Catholic faith on the constant achievements of human knowledge, to which it tries to contribute by its own researches.
3. Fidelity to the message of Christ as it has been handed down by the Church.
4. An institutional commitment to the service of the people of God and the human family on the way to the transcendent goal which gives a meaning to life.[11]

The paragraph concluding this first article of the document could hardly be clearer: 'The realization of these basic conditions decides the Catholic character of a university, whether it has been canonically established or not.'[12] It has to be believed that the essential marks constitute the common denominator in the very diverse categories of Catholic universities in the world.

However, the document does not fail to recognize the existence or the importance of the bonds between the Catholic university and the ecclesiastical authority. It even makes these a criterion for dividing Catholic universities into different categories, though without making them a condition of their Catholic identity. It is interesting to note that the document adds that the Catholic universities which have no statutory link with the ecclesiastical authority are no less Catholic than the others 'whether by the formal and explicit commitment of their founders, the members of their Council or their professors, or by their implicit tradition of fidelity to Catholicism and their social and cultural influence' (no. 15).

After dealing with the government of the university and its activities, the document devotes a last part to its relations with other universities, and immediately before the general conclusion, to its 'relations with the hierarchy of the Catholic Church'. It slightly enlarges on the possible intervention of the ecclesiastical authority, which 'only intervenes if it judges that the truth of the Christian message is at risk' (no. 58). As for 'the form which a possible intervention by the ecclesiastical authorities will take, [this] can vary depending on the type of Catholic institution in question. Where legal links are established, the statutes and regulations can provide for modes of intervention by the hierarchy. In a university which is not connected to the ecclesiastical authorities by statutory links, the latter can intervene through a professor as a member of the Church' (no. 59).

By the emphasis that it puts on the right and duties of the competent ecclesiastical authority to intervene, it seems that the Code was going to provide for the most urgent matters. It left to *Ex corde Ecclesiae* the task of completion, introducing the nuances, distinctions and precisions that 'The Catholic University in the Modern World' did not and, given its nature, could not make.

## III.  The Catholic identity of the university according to *Ex corde Ecclesiae*

In the part relating to doctrinal considerations, the apostolic constitution repeats in full the four essential characteristics which every Catholic university must possess *qua* Catholic (no. 13), according to the document 'The Catholic University in the Modern World' cited above. But the constitution does not go on to add that these characteristics are enough for a university to qualify as Catholic, whether or not it has been canonically established. Without doubt this omission signifies that material or internal elements are not enough to determine the Catholic character of a university. Furthermore the Pope is careful to add, again in the doctrinal part: 'While affirming itself as a university, every Catholic university maintains a relationship with the Church which is essential to its institutional identity' (no. 27).

However, it is for the bishops to give form to this relationship with the university. The Pope recalls that 'even if they do not intervene directly in the internal government of the university, the bishops must not be considered as external agents but rather as participants in the life of the Catholic university'.[13]

The doctrinal part of the apostolic constitution is evidently fundamental, in that it lays the foundations for the normative part. However, it is this latter which constitutes the legislation to be applied in each university concerned.

It is clear from the *Normae generales* which are addressed to existing and future universities with different degrees of retroactiveness that the internal or material characteristics proper to Catholic identity are not sufficient ground for a university to describe itself as Catholic. There must also be external or formal elements which were not considered essentials in the document studied earlier: 'A Catholic university, *qua* catholic, is inspired by Catholic ideals, principles and attitudes in the research which it undertakes, in its teaching, and in all its other activities. It is united to the Church either by a constitutive bond and formal statute or by reason of an institutional commitment undertaken by its authorities' (art. 2 §2).

The other norms are consequences of Catholic identity:

– the public declaration of its character in an appropriate document;[14]
– all the activities of the university must be inspired by Catholic teaching and doctrine, while respecting the freedom of conscience of each person (art. 2 §4);
– every official act of the university must be in accord with its Catholic character (ibid.).

The characteristics proper to Catholic identity mentioned so far relate to every Catholic university existing at the time of the apostolic constitution. They will clearly also have to identify new foundations. However, the constitution also devotes an article specifically to 'The establishment of a Catholic university' (art. 3), which lays down the norms to be followed if such an institution is to be established.

The first two paragraphs do not cause any difficulties. The first recognizes, as did art. 1 §3 for existing universities, the Holy See, the conference of bishops and the diocesan bishop as competent authorities for establishing or approving a Catholic university. The second applies to the establishment of a Catholic university by a religious institution or by another public juridical person the requirement already existing in the Code (see c. 801) for the foundation of an educational institution, namely the consent of the diocesan bishop.

The third paragraph of article 3 poses a problem of interpretation. Having mentioned that other ecclesiastical or lay persons can establish a Catholic university, the text adds that 'this university can only be considered (*poterit haberi solummodo*) a Catholic university with the agreement of the competent authority, according to the conditions agreed by the parties'. At first sight this is a new prescription compared with the Code, which at c. 808 provides that 'Even if it may be Catholic, no university may bear the title or name *Catholic university* without the consent of the competent ecclesiastical authority.'

According to Provost,[15] the norm of *Ex corde Ecclesiae* must be interpreted in the light of the Code; it would thus appear to be a reaffirmation of c. 808. However, the question remains complex and can be envisaged differently. In fact *Ex corde Ecclesiae* can contain a new norm, since article 3 relates to the future of a Catholic university, while c. 808 speaks of a university which is 'really Catholic', i.e. which would already exist. That would mean that in future not only would the consent of the ecclesiastical authority be required for a new university to bear the name or title Catholic, but it would also have to be considered Catholic. By whom? By the founders, by the competent authority, by the community? The text does not say. However, the right to be Catholic *de facto* remains intact. It remains open whether a Catholic university *de facto* is really Catholic, even if it is not so legally.

If that is the significance of article 2 §2, this new norm considerably reduces the possible scope of the initiative sanctioned by c. 216, at least as far as founding a Catholic university is concerned. That is, unless this is a restrictive interpretation of c. 808, which would amount to the same thing. It must be recalled that c. 301 §1 already reserves 'to the competent ecclesiastical authority alone [the right] to establish associations of faithful who propose to teach Christian doctrine in the name of the Church . . .' There would then be a certain coherence between these two norms, even if their immediate object is different.

## Conclusion

In the introduction to *Ex corde Ecclesiae*, John Paul II emphasizes that it is 'necessary to provide Catholic universities with a reference text which can be a Magna Carta for them' (no. 8). The apostolic constitution is more than a 'reference text' from one point of view, constituting a major document above all on the criteria which identify Catholic universities.

But the constitution is far more than a supplement to former documents, whether official or not. Its general norms are 'based on the Code of Canon Law, of which they constitute an extension' (art. 1 §1). They are true laws. Thus art. 1 §1 prescribes the application of the norms contained in the constitution 'to all Catholic universities and institutes of higher study throughout the world. They can be seen among other things in the obligation to indicate their Catholic identity in one way or another (cf. art. 2 §3).

The majority of universities established canonically and with a long Catholic tradition will see no difficulty here, either because they already apply these norms or because some of them will be received as natural supplements. The legislator is well aware that the circumstances of the places where Catholic universities have been established vary considerably from one country or region to another. In the United States, for example, there is a fear that the integral application of these norms will lead to a withdrawal of financial subsidies from the federal government. Already during the 1970s cases to this effect were being brought before the United States Supreme Court to verify the constitutionality of the grants to institutions of higher education connected with the Church.[16]

With the aim of applying the general norms of the apostolic constitution *Sapientia christiana*, John Paul II has given the Congregation for Catholic Education the task of revising the *ordinationes*, the ordinances which are like instructions in the terms of 34 §1. Taking note of the great diversity in local circumstances, the Pope has decided that the redaction of the ordinances with a view to the concrete application of the general norms contained in *Ex corde Ecclesiae* shall be entrusted to the conferences of bishops 'in conformity with the Code of Canon Law and complementary legislation, taking account of the statutes of each university or institute and also – when this is possible and opportune – of civil law' (art. 1 §2).

However, the redaction of these ordinances cannot be done in just any way. They have to conform to the directive issued by the Congregation for Catholic Education on 21 January 1991, addressed to the conferences of bishops with a view to guiding them in this task. These directives will allow the Congregation to save time, since once they are laid down by the conference of bishops, the ordinances must be sent to the Holy See to be 'inspected' (*post inspectionem Sanctae Sedis*).

The question we may now ask relates to the choice that some Catholic institutions may make, no longer to be recognized as such in order to dispense themselves from applying the norms of the apostolic constitution and thus forfeiting some other advantage which might well affect their survival. At all events this is what makes a member of the episcopal committee of the Conference of American Bishops charged with the redaction of the ordinances remark: 'I think that it would be a tragedy if many of our colleges and universities came to speak of themselves as being institutions of higher learning in the Catholic tradition, but having no formal institutional link with the Church.''[17]

*Translated by John Bowden*

## Notes

1. Cf. P. Valdrini, 'Les universités catholiques: exercice d'un droit et contrôle de son exercice (canons 807–814)', *Studia canonica* 23, 1989, 449–52.
2. *Acta Apostolicae Sedis* (*AAS*) 71, 1979, 497–9.
3. The apostolic constitution *Deus scientiarum Dominus*, *AAS* 23, 1931, 241–62.
4. *AAS* 82, 1990, 1475–1509. Cf. *La documentation catholique* (*DC*) 72, 1990, 934–45.
5. Cf. Preamble, III, *AAS*, p. 472.
6. *Periodica* 62, 1973, 625–57. In the presentation, it is stated that this is neither a document of the Federation nor a document of the Congregation for Catholic Education, but is the work of the delegates of the Catholic universities of the world who met in Rome from 20–29 November 1972.
7. Letter of the Sacred Congregation for Catholic Education, ibid., 659.
8. c. 810 §1. This same text presupposes that the statutes of the university would provide a procedure for dismissal if a teacher did not respect these conditions.
9. c. 812. This norm has been the occasion of a most animated debate, above all among American Catholic universities. See among others: A. Gallin, 'On the Road Toward a Definition of a Catholic University', *The Jurist* 48, 1988, 553–5; J. Provost, 'Canonical Aspects of Catholic Identity in the Light of *Ex corde Ecclesiae*', *Studia canonica* 25, 1991, 189–90; L. Orsy, 'The Mandate to Teach Theological Disciplines: Glosses on Canon 812 of the New Code', *Theological Studies* 44, 1983, 476–88; S. A. Euart, 'Implications of Canon 812 for Federal Constitutionality of Government Aid to Catholic Colleges and Universities', *The Jurist* 50, 1990, 167–97; J. A. Coriden, 'The Teaching Office of the Church (cc. 747–833)', in J. A. Coriden, T. J. Green, D. E. Heintschel, *The Code of Canon Law: A Text and Commentary*, commissioned by the Canon Law Society of America, Mahwah 1985, 571–2, 575–6.
10. For the history of the document see Gallin, 'Toward a Definition' (n. 9), 540–4. For a commentary on the part of the document relating to the different categories of Catholic university depending on their connection with the ecclesiastical authority see Valdrini, 'Universités catholiques' (n. 1), 451–8.
11. No. 1, p. 628.
12. Ibid.
13. Ibid., no. 28, *AAS*, p. 1491; *DC*, p. 938.
14. The competent ecclesiastical authority can give a dispensation from this prescription (ibid., 3).
15. Provost, 'Aspects' (n. 9), 176–9.
16. Cf. Gallin, 'Toward a Definition' (n. 9), 548.
17. J. Malone, 'Reflections on Applying the Apostolic Constitution', *Origins* 23, 1993–4, 474.

# Pastoral Care from a Roman Catholic Perspective

## Robert D. Duggan

The question of whether or not there is a specifically 'Catholic' (in the sense of denominational or confessional) notion of pastoral care is an intriguing one. Since Trent, has there developed a distinctively Catholic way of understanding and engaging in the ancient practice of *cura animarum*? And, if so, what has Vatican II done to alter that notion? Is it possible, in an exploration of the broad topic of 'Catholic identity', to discern how the current Catholic praxis of pastoral care is contributory to that identity? And, how does Catholic pastoral care fit within the broad framework of Christian religions as our version of it is manifested in various expressions of local churches around the globe? In the scope of a brief article we surely cannot answer all of these questions. Nonetheless, my hope is to explore the topic sufficiently to elucidate the framework within which these questions may find answers,

The contemporary understanding of Catholic pastoral care, as it has emerged in the wake of Vatican II, has elements of Tridentine particularity as well as a more ecumenically enriched inclusivity. The anti-ritualistic bias of many of the churches of the Reformation served to reinforce a distinctively Catholic emphasis on sacrament. The sort of dichotomous thinking fostered by a Protestant emphasis on *sola scriptura* favoured a focus on the ministry of the Word as the locus for authentic pastoral care. Hence, the eventual narrowing of the notion of pastoral care in Protestant circles to an individualistic, therapeutic model that can operate virtually without reference to the community's sacramental life. At the same time, the Tridentine Catholic reaction cultivated an almost exclusively clerical and ritualistic model of pastoral care which, at worst, rightly deserved the criticisms heaped on a narrowly *ex opere operato* mentality of sacramental ministry.

Any number of historical studies are available tracing the clericalization of sacramental ministry over the course of centuries. Similarly, there are numerous studies detailing the way in which an increasingly legalistic approach characterized Catholic sacramental praxis from the Middle Ages onward. Pastoral care in the post-Tridentine church was heir to both of these trends. As in so many other areas of Catholic identity, what Vatican II accomplished in the area of pastoral care was a freeing of the bonds imposed by a polemical stance and an opening to horizons that are truly ecumenical. The result has not been a break with tradition; rather, an evolution in the Catholic understanding of pastoral care has resulted in a broader and more balanced praxis in the post-Vatican II era. The groundwork for this more open stance was laid in the last century with a developing reflection on 'practical theology' as a separate but respected discipline alongside systematics or dogmatics. In the context of a richer ecclesiological base, it was possible to explore pastoral theology as a part of practical theology. This meant that pastoral theology was able to deal with questions foundational to Christian ministry, rather than with just training individual pastors in the ministerial arts. The way in which both Catholic ecclesiology and sacramental theology have remained in dialogue and contributed to one another's respective evolution for more than a century has also been of immense benefit for a more informed pastoral care praxis at the present time. And, of course, one cannot overlook the many ways in which the teachings of Vatican II have resulted in new theological and pastoral horizons from which contemporary Roman Catholic pastoral care draws for inspiration. It would be well beyond what can be covered in this article to name in detail all of the ways that Vatican II has made those contributions. In its great ecclesiological documents, its vision of liturgy and sacrament, its treatment of the ministry of bishops and priests, and in its teachings on the laity and their call to holiness in the world, one can find the nucleus of the current Catholic understanding of pastoral care.

In attempting to describe an authentically Roman Catholic notion of pastoral care at the present time, it is important to choose judiciously the sources for such a portrayal. Many experiments and creative initiatives are being taken in this age of pluralism, not all of which can serve as representative of a pastoral care that is thoroughly 'Catholic'. Particularly when one seeks to articulate a praxis that can contribute to formal Catholic identity, it is imperative that one seek to establish a certain legitimacy for the model being proposed. In this context, it seems one could not do better than to draw upon the *lex orandi* of Vatican II in the form of the revised sacramental rituals. Embedded in the rites and their *praenotanda* are a fairly clear and consistent vision of Catholic pastoral care, what it presupposes and how it is to be carried forward as part of the Church's ministerial mandate. Many students of Vatican II's liturgical reform feel that the most mature and developed of the revised sacramental rituals is the *Rite of Christian Initiation of Adults*. Some have even made a persuasive case for a kind of normative status that this document enjoys in Catholic sacramental polity. Perhaps no one has spoken more forcefully to this claim than Aidan Kavanagh:

> Rather than regarding the sacraments as separate entities, each containing a meaning exclusive to itself and apart from all others, the full rites of adult initiation presume that all the initiatory rites form one closely articulated whole which relates intimately with all the other non-initiatory sacraments and rites. The entire sacramental economy is thus viewed not as something divorced from and peripheral to Church life, but as the very way in which that life is lived in common and on the most crucial level. The vision is one in which a sacramental theology and an ecclesiology mate to become functions of one another, producing in the concrete a church order of a particular (in this case Roman) kind (127).
>
> All a Christian's rights, privileges, and duties originate here [in the 'economy' established in Christian initiation]. Here the Church's mission is constantly being set at the most fundamental level. Here the obligations to service and the limits on power and authority are established for all ministries within the Church, ordained or not. Initiation defines simultaneously both the Christian and the Church, and the definition is unsubordinated to any other except the Gospel itself, no matter from what source other definitions may originate. This being the case, theological discourse, canonical reform, religious education, ministerial training programmes and even the practical day-to-day running of dioceses and parishes will find it impossible not to take the present document [*The Rite of Christian Initiation of Adults*] as their starting point (*The Shape of Baptism: The Rite of Christian Initiation*, New York 1978, 145).

It would be difficult to find a stronger assertion than this concerning the normative status of the *Rite of Christian Initiation for Adults* for a Catholic notion of pastoral care. What, then, does this document tell us of how the post-Vatican II Church sees *cura animarum*? First and foremost, it is clear that the community is the matrix from which all pastoral care emerges. Far from the hierarchical vision of Trent, which traced the mandate of Christ to the apostles, then to their successors the bishops, and finally to their helpers the priests, it is clear now that the entire community of the baptized carries the responsibility for pastoral care. Where previously the laity were only on occasion and at the discretion of the priest called to assist him in *his* priestly ministry, the *Rite of Christian Initiation of Adults* pointedly indicates that it is the community *qua* community that has been empowered with the Spirit for the sake of ministry. Pastoral care is not something a priest may choose to share with the laity. It is their birthright in baptism and it is their inescapable responsibility, precisely inasmuch as they are called to discipleship in the sacraments of initiation.

There are profound implications of this primacy of the community as the locus of pastoral care. Discernment of pastoral need, equipping individual ministers with the skills needed for specific pastoral care ministries, ongoing support – in myriad forms – for the caregivers, linking pastoral care activities to the celebrations of the liturgical assembly, all of these and more are no longer the exclusive domain of clergy. Rather, they become part and parcel of the normal way that the faithful live out their baptismal identity. This represents a profound shift from the pre-Vatican understanding of pastoral care as a function of the clerical state. Where once priests were called to holiness through the exercise of their pastoral ministry on behalf of the faithful and holiness for the laity was tied into that vision of being the recipients of the priest's (usually sacramental) care, now holiness for all of the baptized is found in exercising their baptismal vocation of pastoral care. The change in identity, from perceiving themselves as the objects of pastoral care to its subjects, is as profound a paradigm shift as any that Vatican II may have triggered.

Closely linked to this new self-perception is an altered perspective as to who is the active subject celebrating the sacramental rituals of the community. Clearly, there is a new-found awareness at this level also: not the priest alone, but the entire assembly is the source of the Church's prayer. The close connection that has traditionally existed between pastoral care and ritual celebration has been heightened by this new ownership of all the faithful. The *Rite of Christian Initiation of Adults* gives explicit ritual expression at many points to the pastoral care exercised by the faithful. Sponsors are asked and promise to watch over their catechumens; based on their own discernment, the faithful are consulted about and ritually acclaim the readiness of catechumens for baptism in the *Rite of Election*. Catechists are deputed to preside over liturgies of the Word, minor exorcisms and blessings.

In the *praenotanda* of virtually all of the revised sacramental rituals, this inextricable connection between pastoral care and ritual celebration is spelled out time and time again. One has only to think of the sacrament formerly known as 'extreme unction' to see this connection at work in its

most expressive form. Now, even the title of the ritual book carries a
reference to the pastoral care of the community for those to be anointed.
The *praenotanda* clearly spell out the connection between ritual anointing
and the community's care for the sick in their midst. That care takes many
forms: ritually, there is encouragement for an expanded eucharistic
ministry to the sick and homebound. Similarly, prayers are provided
which suggest how important a ministry it is to be a companion to the sick
in the course of their illness. Pastoral care in the form of compassionate
presence is linked explicitly with Jesus' own concern for those who suffer.
A broad understanding of this notion of being companion to the sick is
obvious in the ritual. It includes the various ways that the faithful are called
to remain present to the sick during their struggle with physical, emotional
and spiritual suffering. When the sick wrestle with a God who seems to
have turned a deaf ear, or when they totter on the brink of despair, then
pastoral care often takes the form of personal presence, perhaps by a
wordless solidarity in suffering, perhaps by actually speaking the words of
the ancient psalms of lament which fill the ritual book. Even the person to
be anointed, whom one might expect to be described as the object of the
Church's ministrations, is portrayed as taking an active part both in the
liturgy of anointing and in the struggle with suffering that is celebrated
through the ritual prayers. In what approaches mystical insight, the sick
person – immersed in Christ's paschal mystery through suffering – is
presented as one who exercises pastoral care for the community through
faith-filled witness. The true challenge of pastoral care that the community
faces is how to support and enable that kind of active response on the part
of the one who is ill. The healing aimed at by pastoral care always results in
one who is able to minister (even by example) in the community in more
faithful and committed ways.

   If one were to look for what it is that distinguishes the Roman Catholic
notion of pastoral care from the understandings prevalent in Protestant
churches, two characteristics would stand out most strongly. The first
would be what I have described above as the communal context for all
pastoral care, and the second would be the close linkage that exists between
pastoral care and ritual celebration. There is one final feature of Catholic
pastoral care in the post-Vatican II era that we share in common with our
Protestant sisters and brothers. In fact, it is an emphasis that we perhaps
have learned by listening to the Protestant experience more closely and
with a more open mind. It is that pastoral care is ultimately about a
conversion of heart and mind to Jesus Christ, a conversion that results in a
life more committed to God's work and the Church's mission. In his
valuable book *A Roman Catholic Theology of Pastoral Care* (Philadelphia

1983), Regis Duffy develops this understanding at some length. He, too, points to the *Rite of Christian Initiation of Adults* as an invaluable guide to the shape of authentic pastoral care.

In the catechumenal process it is clear that conversion is a gradual, progressive process which is supported and fostered by the community's many forms of pastoral care for the catechumen. In a similar fashion, Catholic pastoral care is an ongoing process in which the community calls its many and various members to conversion and mature faith. Just as it ministers to catechumens who are preparing for the sacraments of Christian initiation in ways that are meant to result in committed discipleship, so the community ministers to the already initiated in a variety of ways with the same ultimate aim. The *Rite of Penance* and its associated pastoral care strategies are all about a lifelong process of ongoing conversion. Similarly, the two sacraments of vocation (marriage and orders) and the extended pastoral care associated with them, both by way of preparation for them and by way of continuing support throughout a lifetime, are ultimately about how we as a community call one another to transformed lives stamped indelibly with the image of Christ. Authentic pastoral care announces that discipleship, lived out in the commitment of a lifelong vocation, requires a creative fidelity that must be grounded in ongoing conversion. Those who offer pastoral care to one whose fidelity to a priestly or married vocation seems to flag in times of crisis know well the role of personal conversion in sustaining and renewing that original commitment.

There is much more that could be added in describing the contours of pastoral care as the post-Vatican II Roman Catholic Church has come to know it. However, what has been presented thus far should offer a satisfactory framework for the exploration of those further dimensions. I hope that I have shown that there does indeed seem to be a distinctively Roman Catholic praxis of pastoral care at the present time which can be glimpsed through the broad categories offered above. How that praxis contributes to the larger question of Catholic identity should be possible to trace through the other articles in this issue.

# III · Ecumenical Dimension

# Roman Catholic Identity amid the Ecumenical Dialogues

## David Tracy

### I. Introduction: the three elements of Roman Catholic identity

The important dialogues of Roman Catholics and the other major Christian churches have yielded enormous fruit. Like many theologians, it is my hope that the remarkable theological agreements achieved in true dialogues will be accepted throughout the Christian churches. Any agreement based upon the kind of theological care and acuteness in those dialogues deserves not merely the encouragement but the strong endorsement of all serious ecumenical Christians. It is dialogue with others, moreover, which helps any careful thinker to rediscover one's own identity. Sometimes, indeed, only such dialogue can help one discover that identity – as if for the first time.

Rather than attending to the many important and well-known specific theological, doctrinal and church order issues resulting from the dialogues, this article will step back to observe the more general question of Roman Catholic identity in the midst of these ecumenical dialogues. To achieve this more general aim, the analysis will take the following form: first a return to two modern Catholic and ecumenical thinkers – John Henry Cardinal Newman and Baron Friedrich von Hügel – for their classic analyses of the fuller complexity of the question of Roman Catholic identity; second some further reflections informed by contemporary ecumenical dialogues on each of the three components (the institutional, the intellectual and the life of piety) constituting Roman Catholic identity as Catholic.[1]

Newman's reflections of the reality of the Church bear a distinctly Catholic mark. When Newman appealed to the 'idea' of the Church, he understood 'idea' as one's deepest sense of the concrete whole and its constituent parts at once. Like so many in his age, 'idea', for him, meant not an abstraction from reality but the reality itself as spiritually sensed and partially but never fully understood. In his *Essay on the Development of Doctrine* Christianity itself was such an organic idea: sensed, felt, understood, and yielding itself to partial, incomplete, but true understanding as it developed through the centuries. The Church, as an idea, was the objective reality of the Body of Christ, constituted by the Spirit of Christ. That is why only the truly spiritual could understand the Church, and why the Christian experienced the understood Christ and the Spirit in and through the Church.

The idea of the Church was never for Newman a mere idea but the polity which is the Church existing here and now: the one Catholics live in, whose gifted reality, as well as human faults and need for self-reform, is always there. It is a part, therefore, of Catholic spirituality to sense and understand the Church in its unity and in its distinct parts – parts that can never efface the antecedent divinely graced unity. It is also part of Catholic spirituality to struggle to discern what part of the Church now needs strengthening, or development, or correction of excesses by reform. The temptation of the prophetical teaching office (theology) is rationalism; that of the ruling office is power; that of the sacred ministry and piety is superstition. Each temptation needs to be discerned and healed, and the danger of each part thinking itself the whole Church needs to be avoided. Thus could Newman appeal to history when, in the fourth century, most of the bishops abandoned the true christological doctrine in the Arian controversy and the Church depended on the laity to maintain its true identity. This example impelled Newman to insist on the need to consult the laity and to defend the *sensus fidelium* as a truly ecclesial sense.

In sum, for Newman doctrine, sacrament, tradition, community and, above all, Church as Body of Christ comprising three equally indispensable functions form the spirituality of Catholics in all cultures. This formation allows a great diversity of spiritual ways while uniting them in the central reality of the Spirit's indwelling presence to the individual soul in communion with Church as the spiritual presence of Christ. Newman's exceptional sensitivity to the need for diversity and powers of discernment in the ever-shifting historical and theological reality of the Church made his spirituality influential for many modern Catholics as both unmistakably Catholic and clearly modern. That same spiritual sense pervades the openness to the good in other religious traditions and to the best of modernity in the major decrees of the Second Vatican Council and the recent ecumenical dialogues.

One major example of the influence of Newman on his younger contemporaries may be found in the thought of Baron Friedrich von Hügel.[2] Although perhaps mostly remembered for his complex role in the Modernist crises of the early twentieth century, Baron von Hügel's contribution to modern Catholic spirituality is found in his classic work, *The Mystical Element of Religion as Studied in Saint Catherine of Genoa and Her Friends*.

Von Hügel's own work may be viewed as a genuinely modern development of Newman's insight into Catholic diversity-in-unity. Von Hügel applied that Newmanian insight not solely to the reality of the church but to the reality of religion itself. Von Hügel was far less theological than Newman and less concerned, therefore, with showing the theological reality of the Church as the presence of Christ's indwelling Spirit. His principal concern was to develop a philosophy of religion that could show the actuality of the concrete person as a unity-in-diversity and thereby the actuality of religion itself as having the character of a concrete person with both great multiplicity and real unity.

Philosophically, von Hügel (in harmony with the radical empiricism and personalism of his period) developed a personalist philosophy that argued for the presence of emotional, intellectual and volitional elements acting in harmony in every person. He believed, as did Coleridge and Newman before him, that a prior unity is given to any concrete personal reality. That reality can be sensed and lived but never fully analysed. One can, however, note the need for the complex development of each person for the full development and harmonization of the emotional, intellectual and volitional elements.

This personalist model deeply informs von Hügel's discussion of religion in *The Mystical Element of Religion*. There he attempts to show, on the occasion of a historical study of the action-in-the-everyday spirituality of St Catherine of Genoa, that every living religion bears its clearest analogue in the living person. The believer knows and trusts the concrete reality of God disclosed in the religion. As with a person, the living unity and trust are concretely realized before analysis and criticism are forthcoming. Analogous to the emotional, intellectual and volitional elements in the person, religion exercises three principal functions. It continuously needs to develop each element and its interrelationships to the other elements to achieve the balance and harmony of an authentic personality.

This personalist analogy led von Hügel to his promising suggestion for understanding the three major elements comprising a historical religion. He employed various phrases for this distinction. One of them insists that every concrete religion comprises three elements: 1. 'the external, authoritative, historical, traditional and institutional element' (analogous to the volitional element in the person); 2. 'the critical-historical and synthetic-philosophical element' (analogous to the intellectual); and 3. 'the mystical and directly operative element of religion' (analogous to the emotional).

Von Hügel attempted, above all, to be faithful to the complexity of Catholic Christianity while also attending to some peculiarly modern intellectual needs. Examples of von Hügel's combination of Catholic balance and modernity are seen in the following: 1. the 'institutional' element is real and to be affirmed, but only as related to the necessary fullness of this 'external' element more fully described as authoritative, historical and traditional; 2. the 'intellectual' element is crucial and now, in the modern period, must include not only the philosophical-synthetic (as in the classic scholastic theologies and their less happy – for von Hügel – neo- scholastic successors) but also the critical-historical (as in biblical and doctrinal studies); 3. the 'mystical' element is not merely passive, but includes a note of action as well – as the spirituality of Catherine of Genoa shows; as, indeed, for von Hügel the most representatively Catholic mystical spiritualities (as incarnational) are also action-oriented in principle.

What Newman attempted to show under the theological rubric of Church, von Hügel addressed under the philosophical rubric of 'religion'. Both can be considered classic modern reflections in Catholic identity in an ecumenical setting. Both insist that God's reality is mediated in the concrete historical form of Church (Newman) and religion (von Hügel). Only attention to that concreteness as sensed by the believer assures both the personalism and the objectivity essential in Catholic identity. Both acknowledge that this unity occurred in great spiritual diversity: a diversity occasioned by different temperaments, cultures and historical periods and a diversity grounded in the triple office of the Church (Newman) or the threefold elements of concrete religion (von Hügel). Both insisted that in Catholic identity this sense of God's reality is mediated to us in Jesus Christ and the Church. Both also insisted on the constant spiritual need for Catholics to discern critically corrections and developments of these three functions as well as the contributions and promise of modernity for Catholic self-understanding.

## II. The three elements of Roman Catholic identity and their continuing reform

Since the renewal of the Church's spirit and structures in the Second Vatican Council, several new images and models have been used to express further these insights on Catholicism and its identity.[3] First, consider the institutional element in the midst of the new images for Church. What first strikes any observer of the Catholic Church is the phenomenon of its sheer 'lasting-power' and size as an institution. The model or image of the Church as institution is both true to the fact of the Church's historical life and an authentic model or image for many important aspects of that life. Viewing the Church as institution, one can understand its social reality and its use of various institutional forms in various periods of history: for example, the Church's use of corporation theory in the mediaeval period; the use of the 'perfect society' model in the Tridentine period; and the use of the model of collegiality in Vatican II. The effectiveness of the Church's transnational commitment to social justice in the world, for example, continues to depend largely upon its ability to remain a cohesive and vital institution which witnesses a common spirit. The effectiveness of its commitment to its own internal reform also depends upon continued incorporation of its own collegiality model into its internal institutional forms. The institutional model remains, therefore, a vital factor in the Church's self-understanding. Its continuing reform remains urgent and the ecumenical dialogues clearly show.

Four other models employed since Vatican II have proved especially helpful in highlighting various aspects of the Church's life. They are: the Church as mystical communion; as sacrament; as herald; and as servant and prophet. When we speak of the Church as 'mystical communion' we mean to affirm that it is and will always remain not merely a human institution but a mystery as profound as all the other central mysteries of God's self-revelation in Jesus Christ. The social reality of the Church is also the social reality of a common union (a 'communion') grounded in the mystery of God's action in Jesus. Following St Paul, the Church uses the image of the mystical body to describe this social reality of our union in and with Christ. Again following the Scriptures, the Second Vatican Council helped Catholics realize that reality more deeply by proclaiming the liberating image of the Church as the people of God. These images alert one, as institutional language alone cannot, to the fact that the Church is ultimately a mystery grounded in Jesus Christ enlivened by his Spirit. As Newman and von Hügel insisted, therein lies a grounded Catholic identity.

The image or model of the Church as sacrament of the encounter with God allows one to unify the insights of the first two models. To speak of the Church as 'sacrament' suggests both its incarnate and institutional reality and its mysterious reality as Christ's presence in the world. By using the model or image of 'herald', the Church wishes to emphasize its character as an event: as the actual congregation of those faithful to God's word, gathered together by the preached word itself. The Church is never more the Church than when gathered together at the eucharist to hear God's word and celebrate the sacraments in each local church. The recent emphasis upon the Church as herald of the good news of the gospel and upon the 'local church' (possibly inspired by the dialogues) is a striking reminder that no matter how wide the vision, nor how universal the commitments, the Church is in the first place 'church' in the local community where the eucharist and word are celebrated.

Each model or image allows for another and distinctive glimpse into the reality of the Church. In affirming the Church as institution Catholics affirm its social reality and effectiveness. In affirming the Church as mystical body and people of God they affirm that their deepest union as a people is communion in the radical mystery of God's gift in Jesus Christ. In affirming the Church as sacrament Catholics recall how the Church makes present anew that mystery in words, actions, symbols and sacraments. In affirming the Church as herald of the gospel they recall how the experience of the Church is rooted in, indeed incarnate in, the local church's fidelity to the gospel and celebration of the eucharist.

But not even all these rich images and models for understanding the Church exhaust its reality. The Church in the modern world has also emphasized its role as servant to humanity and prophet to humanity. As the great liberation movements around the world have shown, the Church is also the servant of humanity, especially of the poor and the oppressed, and should be prophet concerning the real needs of the day. The model of image of the servant Church reminds Catholics that the Church is not closed in upon itself, not called to a triumphalism over the world. Rather the Church as Church, in fidelity to Jesus Christ as the Suffering Servant, is called to turn out towards the world and to suffer for and with the poor and the oppressed.

The image or model of the Church as a prophetic witness to humanity recalls that the Church has the authentic vocation of the prophets of the Old Testament. In fidelity to Jesus Christ, the Church is not called simply to applaud the powers that reign nor to bless the *status quo*. Rather, it should also perform a truly critical and prophetic function. By employing the rich religious resources of the Old and New Testament prophetic traditions and the resources from faith and reason of its own tradition of social justice, the Church must speak to the world in judgment upon all these principalities and powers – economic, social, cultural and political – which aid any form of oppression. By understanding itself as servant Church and prophetic witness, the Church declares that, in the realistic yet joyful spirit of the cross and resurrection, Catholics are all called to the struggle for justice, not as an extra avocation but as the concrete embodiment of the Church's true vocation as servant to humanity.

The Church's struggle for justice also involves the creation of just structures and the performance of just actions within the Church itself as the ecumenical dialogues also help to clarity. As the *ecclesia semper reformanda*, the Church always in need of reform, it must be constantly aware of the need to assure just practices and procedures within its own institutional forms. The central principles of the Catholic tradition of social justice – the dignity of every person, the importance of assuring economic, cultural, social and political equality of opportunity for all, the joint principles of subsidiarity and the common good – should be embodied in institutional reforms of the Church's internal practices.

The reforms of the institutional elements of the Roman Catholic tradition continue to need constant attention. The theological contributions to that institutional reform (including the implicit contribution from the ecumenical dialogues) are genuine – as the analysis of the influence of different theological models for Church already suggests. However, the other two 'elements' of Catholic identity (the intellectual and the life of piety or spirituality) also need further reflection.

In the Catholic tradition, part of Catholic intellectual identity is the close relationship between theology and philosophy (and, therefore, between 'faith' and 'reason'). It is difficult to conceive of a strictly Roman Catholic Barthian position. Even the closest contemporary analogue to Barth in Roman Catholic theology, Hans Urs von Balthasar, remains notably Catholic in appeals to philosophy in theology and in his brilliant defences of analogy, aesthetics and form in theology. This insight can lead one to the following generalization: a part of Catholic theological identity is some sense of an affirmation of 'reason' (and thereby philosophy or the philosophical side of the other disciplines) for use in theology. The relationships between theology and philosophy in Catholic identity covers a wide spectrum indeed; but rarely is the position simply confrontational as in Karl Barth or simply dismissive of 'metaphysics' and 'mysticism' as in so many neo-orthodox and even some liberal (A. Ritschl) Protestant theologians.

One of the singular events of the last fifteen years, moreover, is the closer relationship of the 'intellectual' and 'spiritual' elements in Catholic identity: consider, for example, the new relationship developed between Catholic theology and spirituality. Indeed, it is now widely agreed that a distinction between theology and spirituality (unlike the distinction between theology and philosophy) was allowed to become a separation.

That separation of theology and spirituality has proved disastrous to both. Once separated from spirituality, theology is in danger of becoming merely abstract. Theology then begins to offer stones where people want bread. Once separated from theology, spirituality is always in danger of becoming merely sentimental. Spirituality begins to offer cake when people demand bread.

The many attempts to reunite Catholic theology and spirituality (and thereby the 'intellectual' and 'spiritual' elements of Catholic identity), especially those influenced by the ecumenical dialogues, has proved crucial for Roman Catholic identity. This has occurred in two principal ways. First, the traditional Catholic emphasis on sacrament (indeed its sacramental envisionment of all reality) continues as central to any Catholic identity. Now, however, thanks partly to the Roman Catholic-ecumenical dialogues, it is more accurate to speak of the word-sacrament dialectic in Catholic identity. In a similar way, the traditional Catholic theological commitment to an analogical imagination and language (which are, after all, the direct conceptual counterpart of a Catholic religious sacramental vision) now also possesses more dialectical moments, again thanks partly to the ecumenical dialogues.

Secondly, these dialogues have also encouraged the development of new forms of what Gustavo Gutiérrez and others have named a 'mystical-political' spirituality and theology.[4] These political, liberation and feminist theologies have reunited not only theory and praxis but theology and spirituality – and often in an ecumenical manner. Roman Catholic identity is now far more complex and pluralistic than in the past but remains recognizably Catholic. Newman and von Hügel could acknowledge the greater ecumenical diversity in the new forms of unity-in-diversity of a new Catholic identity. The future for Roman Catholic identity remains as promising as its willingness to enrich the institutional, spiritual and intellectual elements in an ever new unity-in-diversity. No small part of that newly emergent Roman Catholic identity will be played by a fuller incorporation of the ecumenical dialogues into further institutional reform, deeper spiritual enrichment and a firmer ecumenical character to all Catholic theology. Surely Roman Catholic identity as both fundamentally Catholic and genuinely – i.e. inclusively – catholic can welcome this.

## Notes

1. I have developed this analysis of Newman and von Hügel further for the question of the unity-in-diversity of Roman Catholic spirituality in 'Recent Catholic Spiritu-

ality: Unity amid Diversity', in Louis Dupré and Don E. Saliers (eds.), *Christian Spirituality III: Post-Reformation and Modern*, New York and London 1989. For the fuller analysis see that article.

2.  On von Hügel, see *The Mystical Element of Religion as Studied in St Catherine of Genoa and Her Friends* (2 vols), London 1908.

3.  See Avery Dulles, *Models of the Church*, New York 1976.

4.  Inter alia, see Gustavo Gutiérrez, *On Job: God-Talk and the Suffering of the Innocent*, New York 1984.

# Catholic Identity as seen by a Partner in the Ecumenical Dialogue

## André Birmelé

'Today Protestant theologians have learned that even with Denzinger and the manuals in hand, it is not so easy to go hunting the high prey. And some can be heard asking, not without irritation, where does this Catholic theology hide out anyway? But the question is a step forward – indicating some realization here of the dynamic and inexhaustible riches in Catholic teaching. In fact, Catholic teaching is too Catholic to be readily spotted in any one place, for it still lays claim to *all* truth.'[1] A theologian from another church tradition seeking to define Roman Catholic theology still remember this statement made by Hans Küng in 1957. It is an indication of the difficulty of our task.

This difficulty is magnified by the complexity of the notion of identity. The identity of a church comprises more than its doctrine. It is the sum of a multitude of elements: historical and doctrinal, geographical and cultural, spiritual and legal, sociological and psychological dimensions combine to form it. Excessive emphasis on one of these aspects soon results in a caricature which betrays the church concerned.

That applies to any Christian family, and it also applies above all to the Roman Catholic family, the Church which understands itself as 'the Catholic Church', the Church in its fullness.

To evoke Roman Catholic identity seems inevitably to introduce a partial and partisan result, as is indicated by all the efforts made by Protestant theologians as well as by Roman Catholic theologians themselves.

## I. Protestant attempts before Vatican II

The history of the theology of the churches which emerged from the Reformation in the sixteenth century is full of examples of authors who tried to define Roman Catholic identity. F.D.E. Schleiermacher was one of the first to launch out on this adventure. He located the difference between the Protestant and the Catholic in the fact that 'the former makes the individual's relation to the Church dependent on his relation to Christ, while the latter contrariwise makes the individual's relationship to Christ dependent on his relation to the Church'.[2] For him this distinction is not only doctrinal, but also ethnic, and expresses the distance between Latin (Roman) and German culture, the former emphasizing in its religious concepts the notions of priests, cults and sacrifices, the latter emphasizing critical and prophetic thought. At the end of the nineteenth century von Harnack locates the difference in the notions of sacraments and word, the one involving a religion of doing and seeing, the other one of hearing. This difference is comparable to that between works and faith, a difference from which it derives.[3] In the twentieth century Tillich speaks of the more prophetic 'Protestant principle' which protests against all forms of religious objectification and in particular against the objectification of grace, the temptation of religion of a sacramental type which Tillich sees in Roman Catholicism. However, this latter remains necessary to Protestantism.[4] Gerhard Ebeling opposes 'church of the sacrament' to 'church of the word', a 'phenomenon with a fundamental hermeneutical difference' which is not only a question of language but the difference between existence before God by the action 'in which one makes something of oneself' and that emphasizing 'faith alone' and the 'Word alone'.[5] Finally, in a letter to the schoolboy Thomas Wipf, Karl Barth brings out seven essential doctrinal differences, though he emphasizes the precarious character of this mode of analysis.[6]

Given the way in which the Reformation churches define themselves, this concentration on one or more specific doctrinal questions should not be surprising. These attempts, all prior to Vatican II, correspond to analogous Catholic attempts (J. A. Möhler, E. Przywara, Y. Congar) to describe the Protestant identity.

## II.  Fruits of the dialogue after the Council

After Vatican II, the Roman Catholic Church chose resolutely to become involved in the contemporary ecumenical movement and with the other Christian traditions to seek a wider communion in the one Church of Jesus Christ. As a result, like all the other confessional families, in the dialogue it was led to specify its own contours, first doctrinal and then more generally ecclesial. After more than thirty years of dialogue, the analyses of the eminent representatives of Protestant theology quoted above have thus been refined.

What does the Roman Church look like in these dialogues? The international Lutheran-Roman Catholic dialogue is significant and gives the Protestant theologian a more precise vision of the Roman Church. In its first phase the dialogue notes a 'broad consensus' on salvation in Christ and the definition of the gospel, 'the proclamation of the saving event by which the salvation is transmitted which God gives to the world through Jesus Christ'.[7] This salvation is not based on any condition to be realized by the believer but is a new reality that is given in the word and the sacrament and that transforms the whole human being. The difference which remains can be summed up in a question: is the justified believer sanctified to the point of being able herself or himself to be the author of a sanctifying act? However, this problem is not a divisive one because behind it lies a basic common vision: all affirm the prior action of God in the saving act. Numerous traditional contrasts (word-sacrament, faith-works) are obsolete.

This agreement and this difference are extended in the later dialogue on ecclesiological questions. The dialogue on the 'Lord's Supper' ended in broad agreement. The questions which remain open are in fact only the ecclesiological translation of the difference brought out in soteriology.[8] In connection with the eucharistic presence, the minister presiding at the celebration and the eucharistic sacrifice, one and the same point always appears: in the Roman Catholic understanding, does not the Church become the author of the eucharist in a way which the Reformation churches can no longer accept? The same goes for the dialogue on the ministries.[9] There is a broad consensus. The particular ministry is essential for the Church. It is at the service of the Word and the sacraments, at the service of Christ, the sole mediator. The difference relates to the way in which this ministry participates in the priesthood of Christ,[10] the particular character conferred by ordination, which leads the Roman Church to note a *defectus sacramenti ordinis* among the Lutherans. The same problem also appears at the level of the Magisterium over the definition of the role of the Church and its Magisterium in the authorized interpretation of scripture, even if all affirm the prior authority of the gospel over every ministerial structure and over the Church. In the more ecclesiological sphere, this difference for the moment remains a divisive factor.

A detailed analysis of the other dialogues in which the Roman Catholic Church is engaged (for example with the Anglicans or the Reformed) would show that in these dialogues, too, the issues which remain controversial are of this order.

The ultimate point on which all the open questions are converging relates to the participation of the Church (and its ministries) in the saving work of God. For all concerned, the instrumentality is secondary compared to the prior instrumentality of God; ecclesial mediation can never be put in parallel to the prior mediation of Christ. The difference relates to the place accorded by one side or the other to the mystery of the Church in the whole of the Christian mystery. In Roman Catholicism, the Church appears more central and its instrumentality more effective than in the traditions which come out of the Reformation, where, while these factors are not absent, they are more secondary. The statement of the Joint French Catholic-Protestant Committee sums up this point by explaining that, for Catholicism, the Church 'is at the service of the mediation of the Christ whom it makes effectively present'.[11] The contentious issue is the interpretation of this 'effectively'. It is in fact a matter of the distinction and the relationship between divine action and human action in the Church. This cannot be summed up in a single doctrinal proposition. Here are tendencies which must be described by means of comparatives, some putting more emphasis on ecclesial co-operation in the saving action of Christ than others.

Thus in the dialogues of these last years, the Roman Catholic Church has defined itself and been understood by its Protestant partners as a Christian family with an original ecclesiological understanding. This different approach to the mystery of the Church in the saving plan of God leads to different expressions of the faith and to particular theological affirmations. However, that has not brought us back to the affirmations of Protestant theologians before Vatican II, since the ecumenical movement has also taught us that these different options are not exclusive. This ecclesiological difference can be perfectly legitimate and can take its place in the context of the fundamental consensus on the saving work of God. It then loses its divisive character, as has been the case in soteriology. The one Church of Christ has difference faces; it is one but not uniform. A complementary theological dialogue should make it possible to go beyond the still divisive character of the difference in ecclesiology by transforming it into a legitimate difference within the fundamental consensus which is not only capable of bearing it but is also expressed through it.[12]

### III.  An understanding of the Church

Concentrated by their very nature on more doctrinal questions, the dialogues have brought out an issue which is not only doctrinal but rather meta-dogmatic: the understanding of the church. It is this point that

Lutheran or Reformed theologians emphasize in their description of
Roman Catholic identity. They affirm with Catholic theologians that the
Church and its institutions participate in the mystery of salvation which
God offers to all humanity, that the Church itself is mystery, the body of
Christ, the communion of believers sharing the same faith, the same Word
and the same sacraments and gathered round the apostolic ministry.
However, they are more reserved when they point out the close link in
Catholicism between the one Church of Christ and the structure of the
Roman Catholic Church, and the way in which the Church and its
structure participate in the work of God.

In dialogue the originality of Roman Catholic identity does not appear so
special because of the doctrinal definitions of the Church, the episcopal or
Petrine ministry, but these definitions simply express a quite specific self-
understanding. The Roman Catholic Church in fact has a vivid awareness
of being the structured body at the heart of society which has a privileged
and particular place in the history of salvation. This structured body
(which is also structured legally, see the Code of Canon Law) is more than
a simple institution. It understands itself as being the mark of the one true
holy, catholic and apostolic church (*nota ecclesiae*), the mother of
believers. It is the expression of the will of God in its actual, organic and
integrative totality. In its visible form it is capable of reform, but
permanent.

This general perception is translated into numerous more specific facts.
Thus where there are tensions, and decisions need to be taken, the ecclesial
structure represented by the ministry has the last word; this understands
itself to have received the charge to be the guarantor of 'being the Church'.
The letter of the Congregation for the Doctrine of Faith on 'Some Aspects
of the Church understood as *Communio*' makes this quite specific by
stating that Christ exercises his prophetic, priestly and royal function
through the hierarchical order of the church. Each local church becomes
'fully Church' thanks to the presence within it of the episcopal college and
in particular the sovereign pontiff.[13] Vatican II was not afraid to say that
'by the will of Christ, the Catholic Church is mistress of Truth', a
statement taken up in John Paul II's recent encyclical *Veritatis splendor*.[14]

It is difficult for non-Catholics to accept that this self-understanding is
only a matter of obedience and not a simple thirst for institutional power.
They have difficulty in grasping its scriptural basis. However, they note
that very different doctrinal options, which in other traditions would
already have led to division, can find their place in this totality thanks to the
amazing integrative power of the Catholic concern to recapitulate everything, keeping it in this one body which understands itself as the keystone

of the diversity. Logically, a break does not occur so much in connection with different doctrinal opinions; it comes when the structure itself is put in question (as it has been by Hans Küng, Leonard Boff and others) and above all when a bishop proceeds to an episcopal ordination not desired by Rome, thus creating a dangerous excrescence for the body itself (as in the case of Mgr Lefèbvre).

Marked for ever by the history of the Reformation in the sixteenth century, Protestant theologians see in this self-understanding the danger of a self-absolutization to the detriment of the gospel. They prefer a church which in its structural and institutional forms understands itself as being more provisional, more historical and more dependent on situations and cultures. Is this church capable of responding to modern challenges, of adapting itself to society, without manifestly betraying its message, which according to the Protestant theologian always precedes every ecclesial expression and is outside the church's control? Numerous examples show that the Roman Catholic Church is capable of adapting itself to the most unforeseen events. However, we can ask whether in an age which more than any other calls for the inculturation of the gospel, this church will be capable of responding to new and justified demands. The recent *Catechism of the Catholic Church* is a good example of this. It is addressed to the bishops and does not require the individual adherence of each believer. Despite that, however, it seems markedly dependent on a Western culture which in many respects seems to be trifling with the truth of the faith. The encyclical *Veritatis splendor* which supplements the *Catechism* in the moral sphere does not hesitate to absolutize certain moral options in the history of the Church. With many Roman Catholic theologians, Protestant theologians question such an approach and stress the imperfection and provisionality of every structure in the Church, an imperfection that Roman Catholicism affirms more readily of 'its members' than of the church itself.[15]

## IV. Mutual recognition

This self-understanding of the Roman Catholic Church leads to a major ecumenical problem: its difficulty in recognizing another ecclesial tradition as an authentic expression of the one Church of Jesus Christ. After years of doctrinal dialogue, it is now time to translate the doctrinal consensus which has been achieved into ecclesial communion. This reception implies the possibility of regarding another ecclesial tradition as Church in the full sense of the word, and thus includes the capacity to relativize its own structural and institutional expression.

There is no denying that the Roman Catholic Church has chosen to engage in ecumenism. In stating that the one Church of Jesus Christ subsists in the Roman Catholic Church and thus putting an end to the simple identification of the two entities, Vatican II took a decisive step.[16] The same nuance is confirmed theologically by the understanding of the church 'in the nature of sacrament'.[17] This theological openness has made possible the developments of the 'Decree on Ecumenism' and in particular the recognition that essential elements of the Church exist outside the visible limits of the Roman Catholic Church. This applies in particular to the Eastern churches, but also to the communities which have emerged from the Reformation. This conviction has never been denied but constantly reaffirmed. The most recent example to date is the 'Ecumenical Directory' of spring 1993, which, while emphasizing the uniqueness of the Roman Catholic Church, confirms that 'the Spirit of Christ does not refuse to make use of them (the other churches and ecclesial communities) as means of salvation'.[18] This attitude is also that of the representatives of the Roman Catholic Church in the dialogue with other traditions, a dialogue the importance of which Rome has never ceased to stress.

In this Christian family, with this openness there co-exists the radical affirmation of Roman Catholic exclusiveness. Here too there are numerous recent examples. We might recall the letter on 'Certain Aspects of the Church understood as *Communio*' or a work like the *Catechism of the Catholic Church* which, while speaking of ecumenism, does not evoke the other churches and their convictions. In the first parts of its report, the 1991 Synod of Bishops for Europe ignores every other ecclesial identity and puts non-Roman Catholic Christians in the same category as Jews or non-Christian believers.[19] The responsibility of Christians for the European continent seems to be the concern only of Roman Catholicism. The same exclusivity appears when it is as a matter of conferring an ecclesial authority on the result of doctrinal dialogue between churches. For example, the Congregation for the Doctrine of Faith has made a negative response to the decisive advances proposed by its own representatives in dialogue with the Anglicans, and in the end simply calls for the return of Anglicans to the Roman Catholic fold.[20] To recognize another church as also being in its differences a full and authentic expression of the one Church of Jesus Christ would seem impossible, since such an attitude would relativize the Roman Catholic identity and in particular its claim to Catholicity.

Consequently, Roman Catholic identity seems marked by an amazing ambiguity. Many elements relativize the claim to exclusiveness traditionally affirmed by Rome, and many facts indicate its persistence. The ambiguity which can be perceived at the level of ecumenical commitment in fact appears when one looks at the actual life of this church, the reactions of its believers, its theologians and its ministers. A relativization of the particular identity and the affirmation of its exclusiveness are often very close to each other, and this extends to the pontifical texts. Thus the last encyclical *Veritatis splendor* states that it is not a matter of imposing a particular option while decreeing that the universal law defined by the Church can only be good for all.[21]

All these elements show a church whose self-understanding no longer fits the evidence, a church which like all the Christian churches is in search of its identity, a church whose certainties are accompanied with doubts, a church which is at this time a true expression of the one Church of Jesus Christ but also one confessional church among others.

*Translated by John Bowden*

## Notes

1. H. Küng, *Justification. The Doctrine of Karl Barth and a Catholic Reflection*, Philadelphia and London 1964, 110f.
2. F. D. E. Schleiermacher, *The Christian Faith*, 1982, para. 24, p. 103.
3. A. von Harnack, *Lehrbuch der Dogmengeschichte*, Tübingen [4]1910, III, 847ff.
4. Paul Tillich, *Gesammelte Werke* VIII, Stuttgart 1962, which contains the articles 'Der Protestantismus als Kritik und Gestaltung' (in particular 29f.) and 'Die beliebende Bedeutung der katholischen Kirche für den Protestantismus' (esp. 132f.).
5. G. Ebeling, *Wort Gottes und Tradition. Studien zu einer Hermeneutik der Konfessionen*, Göttingen 1964, in particular the article 'Worthafte und sakramentale Existenz', 197–216.
6. K. Barth, *Letters: 1961–1968*, Grand Rapids and Edinburgh 1981, 137f.
7. Texts collected in *Face à l'Unité. Tous les textes officiels 1972–1985*, Paris 1986, 29 (para 16 of the Malta Report).
8. 'Le repas du Seigneur', ibid., 61–138.
9. 'Le ministère dans l'Église', ibid., 195–279.
10. Vatican II, *Lumen gentium* 10.
11. *Consensus oecumenique – différence fondamentale*, Paris 1987, para. 12.
12. Cf. the whole study *Grundkonsens-Grunddifferenz*, ed. A. Birmelé and H. Meyer, Frankfurt and Paderborn 1992.
13. Cf. especially paras 4 and 13.
14. John Paul II, *Veritatis splendor*, 64.
15. Vatican II speaks of the imperfection of the Church *in suis membris*, cf. *Unitatis redintegratio* 3, but also of the Church which, embracing sinners in its bosom, is always in need of purification, cf. *Lumen gentium* 8.
16. *subsistit in*, ibid., 8.
17. *quasi sacramentum*, ibid., 1.

18.  A quotation from the decree on ecumenism *Unitatis redintegratio*, in 'Directory on the Application of the Principles and Norms on Ecumenism', *Documentation catholique* 2075/1993, paras 17, 18.

19.  Final Report of the Synod of Bishops for Europe 1991, *Documentation catholique* 2043/1992, 123–32.

20.  Text of this response, ibid, 111–14.

21.  *Veritatis splendor*, 29, 30, 64, 110.

# Future Aspects of Catholic Identity

## Knut Walf

'Catholics do not consider that people's faith also changes, with time and human knowledge. It is impossible for human beings to advance here and stop there. Even truth needs different garb at different times if it is to be helpful.'

'Do you really believe that God is Catholic?'

'The Catholics and the rest.'

(Aphorisms of Georg Christoph Lichtenberg, 1742–1799)

### Different aspects of identity

There are always two sides to identity: on the one hand, a person or an institution can define or establish identity – also, but certainly not only, by law. On the other hand, the identity of a person and an institution is accepted or not, indeed even also shaped, by others. To give an example – several decades ago a university was founded as a Catholic university, and even now its ruling body leaves no doubt that it wants to maintain the Catholic identity of this university. But to the great majority of teachers and students at the university its Catholic identity is a matter of indifference. The main thing is that such a university should function as efficiently as other universities. In such cases identity is concentrated on a label. At all events, among other things by referring to this identity and the corporate freedom of religion guaranteed by the constitution, one can find exceptions from the laws and regulations which apply to all. In the last resort, then, identity is only a desire, in this case more or less only on the part of the ruling body of an institution. But acceptance by others can disappear, be completely absent or no longer exist.

## Identity in church law

Presumably reflection on one's own identity is already a sign of weakness and vanishing identity. When in addition there is an attempt to lay down identity with the help of the law, there may be a crisis of identity for a particular institution. The 1917 Codex had no regulations comparable to those in cc. 216, 300, 803 §3 and 806 of the 1983 codex.[1] In all cases, the source or basis of these regulations is given as no. 24.2 of the Vatican II Decree on the Lay Apostolate *Apostolicam actuositatem* of 18 November 1965.[2] Now church lawyers in particular must raise the justified question whether the law is an appropriate means of guaranteeing the identity of an institution. Behind the regulations of the 1983 Code mentioned above is the mistaken idea of wanting to guarantee the reality by the ideal form of a definition. This phenomenon can in fact often be seen in Catholic church law. But if their laws are to be observed, legislators have to do justice to reality. That means that they must note whether their laws have any chance of being accepted by those to whom they are addressed.

Now when we come to the regulations in the 1983 Code aimed at preserving identity, experience suggests that there is considerable doubt about their sense, and quite particularly about the possibility of the implementation. Thus for example in the Dutch diocese of Roermond the efforts of the former Bishop Gijsen to impose statutes along the lines of his understanding on Catholic schools failed completely, in that he made his permission for them to continue to be called Catholic dependent on c. 803 §3.

## The new social confusion

Given a confused social situation (pluralism) and markedly divergent developments in the particular churches of the Roman Catholic Church, the answer of the church legislator is very simple: the competent church authority establishes who and what is 'Catholic'. This makes the authority competent, but the church legislator in no way has well-founded competence to assign this competence. Had the church legislator stipulated that only the competent church authorities were authorized to state who or which institution was 'Roman Catholic', such a legal norm would have a degree of plausibility. But as this has not happened, in civil processes over the label 'Catholic' it may be difficult for the interests of the so-called Catholic Church to be recognized as compared with persons and institutions. However, recently the legislature in the Federal Republic of

Germany has established that only organizations recognized by the Roman Catholic may bear the designation 'Catholic'.

As the word 'catholic' (Greek = universal) originally already indicates, it is an expression of openness. Up to the Reformation it was the designation of the whole Christian Church. And even today, parts of the Christian Church still use this term to describe themselves, like the Old Catholic Church, the Christian Catholic Church, and so on.

The misunderstandings of this kind, whether intentional or not, began with the *Codex Iuris Canonici* of 1917, the first law book of the 'Catholic' Church. In its c. 100 §1 it laid down that the 'Catholic Church' has the status of a person by law (in CIC 1983 = c. 113 §1). But its c. 1 states that this Codex only extends through the sphere of the Latin Church (thus also succinctly the new Code in c. 1: 'The canons of this Code affect only the Latin Church'). And the Latin Church is also – whether appropriately, we need not discuss here – the Roman Church or the Roman Catholic Church. Thus the 1983 Code speaks of the Pope as the *Romanus Pontifex* (Roman Pontiff, c. 330) or of the cardinals of the holy Roman Church (c. 249). It is evident that the definition is rather confused. However, it should also be clear that the legislators of the Latin Church did not have the essential competence to want to define who or what institution is 'Catholic'. Because of the overlapping in (self-)designations mentioned above, at all events it had the competence to define by law and administrative act which person or institution is 'Roman Catholic' or a part of the Latin Church.

A further dilemma emerges with the term 'Roman'. The central organs of the Latin Church have this word in their designations. In addition to Pope and cardinals the central administrative organ of the whole Church, the Roman Curia (c. 360), bears this adjective, as does the Roman Rota, the ordinary tribunal established by the Pope to receive appeals from the courts of the Catholic or Latin Church (1443). But they are called 'Roman' because they were originally institutions of the Bishop of Rome or the Roman particular church which became universally significant for large parts of the Christian Church as a whole through the historical accrual of the power of jurisdiction to the Bishop of Rome. In other words, institutions of a particular church became central organs of the Church as a whole or the Latin Church. After the Reformation its competence extended exclusively to the Roman Church. This situation is of far-reaching significance for the present awareness of Catholic identity in the Roman Catholic Church as a whole and in its particular churches. For we have to ask to what degree these traditional structures of a specific particular church, namely that of Rome, function to create or preserve identity today and in the different particular churches. More and more doubts and thus problems are arising here which are not necessarily new, but are now becoming much more evident. In short, one can speak of the problem of inculturation.

## The Catholic utopia

Ideally to bring Christian faith of whatever cultural stamp under the unifying roof of Catholicity is an old dream which was never fully realized, since it is utopian. One might recall the famous remark of Vincent of Lérins (who died in 450 near Nice). In his *Commonitorum* (ch. 2.5) we can read: 'It is necessary to strive with all our might to preserve the object of faith, everywhere, always and for all. This is what is truly and authentically Catholic.'[3] Apart from the telling word 'authentically', the statement makes clear this utopian character. Vincent of Lérins indeed also gives his axiom primarily an orientation on the future. As what he postulated was manifestly not the case in his lifetime, he called for this 'authentic' Catholicity to be striven for. But in his axiom there is also the argument from tradition which also shapes Catholicity to such a degree: 'We' are to *preserve*. So in this call we can see a tension comparable to that in squaring the circle.

The aim is quite manifestly Catholicity in the sense of a completely overarching roof. Here Vincent of Lérins presumably expected the universal acceptance of the content of faith. The more the Christian Church developed into a great institution, the more of course elements of organization and legal structure were added which 'one' had (has) to accept if one wanted (wants) to be regarded as a Catholic. Here for example we might refer to c. 205: in addition to the content of faith and the sacraments the church government must also be recognized if a baptized person is to be regarded as 'fully in the communion of the Catholic world'.

## Unity and difference

Looking at history, and also taking into account the laws of institutions, we can constantly see that the potential confusion in an institution increases with its size and complexity. This in turn has to be overcome with the help of regulations (dogmas, laws) if such an institution is to be governable, indeed if it is to go on existing at all. However, general regulations or large-scale structures often fail to take account of particular interests and needs. So far, those large organizations and institutions which for whatever reason allowed diversity in unity (e.g. the Holy Roman Empire under Habsburg rule) have lasted the longest. But at some point even these have disappeared because they were ungovernable or disintegrated from the periphery inwards.

This may well also be the fate of the Roman Catholic Church. It is generally overlooked that the Roman Catholic Church as an apparently closed, global structure has in fact existed at most only since the Counter-Reformation, and in its present form indeed only since the first half of the nineteenth century. Before the Counter-Reformation, over wide areas (e.g. in the German language areas) right down to the nineteenth century the Catholic Church was a composite of more or less independent particular churches with their own traditions, for example in the spheres of liturgy and discipline. For this period one can in some respects speak of a federal church in which, however, over the course of centuries a central dominance by Rome developed. However, for very different reasons (problems of communication, the resistance of secular powers, etc.) Rome could only relatively seldom assert its pre-eminence. In the time before the Reformation or Counter-Reformation the Church was still Catholic, but not Roman Catholic in the present sense. That the Roman unitary model, established not least with the help of a universal lawbook since 1917, is now regarded as the normal or only valid model of the Church could change in the foreseeable future, perhaps in a landslide.

## Vatican II's model of the Church and the change in religion

Vatican II with its ecclesiology of the 'particular churches in which and from which the one and unique Catholic Church exists' (c. 368 on the basis of *Lumen Gentium* 23.1) developed a future model for the Catholic Church or for the catholicity of the Church based on the earlier past (cf. esp. *Lumen gentium* 13.3). However, developments since the Council have moved away from this model, and today the Catholic Church is more remote from realizing it than at the time of the Council.

In view of the declining status of religion in almost all regions of the earth the Catholic model of unity in any case carries greater risks with it than a pluralist model. Religion certainly was and is an export-import item in many cultures and civilizations, but in the long term it can only exist where it has put down deep roots. This gives religion a very indigenous character. Like a veneer, imported religious models can be laid down on religious traditions. But the 'old' religion lives on. And precisely for that reason Catholic religion in a village in the Bolivian hill-country is totally different from that in an Amsterdam suburban community.

The Dutch theologian J. A. van der Ven regards identity as one of the four core functions of the Church; indeed he puts it first, before integration, programme ('beleid')[4] and leadership ('beheer'). He also makes a distinction between the foundations and the identity of the church.[5] The foundations are to be found in the writings of the specific Christian tradition. By contrast, identity is not established but must be constantly formulated anew. On the one hand it changes with the historical and social context in which the church is located. On the other hand, the Church cannot be defined without this context. For a long time, and probably in all cultural circles, a tension has been experienced between a norm once given and historical development. This is attested by the following Chinese text from the third century BCE:

> 'In the land of Chu a man was crossing the Giang. His sword fell out of the ship into the water. Thereupon he made a mark on the ship and said, "This is where my sword fell in." When the ship stopped, he jumped into the water at the point where he had made the mark and looked for his sword.
>
> But whereas the ship had gone on, the sword had not. Is it not therefore foolish to look for the sword in this way? But to seek to enforce the old ordinances in one's kingdom is precisely the same thing. Meanwhile the times have progressed further, but the ordinances have not progressed with them. Would it not therefore be difficult to create order in this way?'[6]

Of course this is also the place to reflect whether 'Catholicity' is attainable at all. In reflecting on Catholic identity, particularly with a view to the future, experience indeed tells us that we must make a realistic estimate as to how far Christian religion can do justice at all to its claim to be a 'world religion'. The existence of this claim, possibly this task, cannot and should not be disputed. But we must also ask just as soberly whether this model of a Western, or more precisely a Western Asian, religion has had or will have any chance at all of worldwide dissemination. No research into causes can be engaged in here. But we should note soberly that apart from those areas in which Islam has established itself as a rival model, large areas of humankind were not and are not ready to adopt the Christian religion: north, east and south-east Asia, large areas of Africa, the so-called Eskimos, and so on. In other parts of the world Christian mission could only be carried on by force, with the consequence that there Christian ideas only lie like a veneer over the old religion (predominantly among the Indians and Indios). Finally, looking into the future, one cannot ignore the current de-Christianization of Europe and North America.[7]

### A realistic model of Catholic identity?

So what would a model of Catholic identity capable of survival look like?[8] Catholic identity with any chance of a future could be a bond between very different regional or even local forms of Catholicity. In this model old, even pre-Christian, forms of religious expression would have to have a legitimate place. New forms of religion would have a chance of existing in such an open model, indeed of being combined with traditional elements.

To return to church law, to church order: it is easy to see that in such a model of Catholic identity an overall framework would have more of a place than a lawbook in the form of the *Codex Iuris Canonici*, with generally very detailed regulations for Catholics in whatever particular church.

On the basis of its tradition the Catholic (Roman Catholic, Latin) Church is a hierarchically divided church, as a whole and in its particular churches. So in a federal church 'the competent church authority' would also have the right to define who is a member or what institution is a part of this church. Nevertheless we shall have to see that an authority which has a closer relation to the traditions, customs and developments than a remote central institution will be able to make such decisions much more appropriately and aptly.

Because of a multicultural environment almost since its beginnings, the Christian Church has had to cope with the tension(s) between *Christian* identity and *cultural* difference, one or other of which has prevailed, depending on the circumstances. As has already been demonstrated, however, Christian or Catholic identity, like any other identity, cannot exist without any relation to the historical or cultural environment, since if it did, it would no longer have a place in a particular human plausibility structure. In that case identity would be fatal, indeed suicidal, 'self-reflection', orientated on the Absolute but with no reference to reality. In philosophical reflexion on identity, one has the differing concept of equality. It would be worth introducing this conceptual distinction into ecclesiology; the Catholic Church is not identical with a Reformation Church, but both exist equally in the Christian tradition. Or, the Catholic Church in the Netherlands is not identical with that in Southern Chile, but they have equal Catholic convictions. This distinction also applies to the historical dimension.

The Church is a community of men and women, of persons. So its identity also determines the identity of these men and women, to the degree that these in turn identify with this Church. In the past attempts were continually made to define positively who could be counted as part of the Church and by what marks of identification. One might think of the definition of Cardinal Bellarmine, which can now be found in c. 205.[9] It can hardly be disputed that already in past times a correspondence between the self-understanding of individual Catholics and the 'self-understanding' of the institutional Church represented a virtually unattainable utopia. From the beginning in Christian communities and later in the Christian Church 'unity' was conjured up, though evidently it was never present. Throughout Christian history the striving for unity and uniformity, for what is distinctively Christian and Catholic and thus identity, has probably been in tension with outside influences which constantly led to syncretistic forms (though these were regularly repudiated) which had to be adopted if Christians did not want to drop out of the general cultural context. Though the content of this faith might have been new, or at least different, the Christian community had to make use of language comprehensible to the people if it was to achieve this. This tension constantly led to conflicts and doctrinal disputes. One need think only of the so-called Rites Controversy in China during the seventeenth century.[10] In today's so-called pluralistic society this problem is in any case immense: the Catholic Church is a mosaic of convictions, generally of a very varied nature. The common denominator may by now have become very narrow, for all the assertions and warnings of the Church's Magisterium. We must simply note an extreme time lag between convictions and experiences which probably can hardly be brought together under one roof, for example an increasingly voluminous World Catechism. Catholic identity will not be achieved or secured if the church government – even with the help of its law – simply constructs a so-called self-referential system which is coherent and thus plausible. The questions and enquiries of the people not only arise from their experiences in the internal sphere of faith and Church but may even have their origin for the most part in experiences 'out in the world'. A great step towards Catholicity, towards Catholic identity, would be the final acceptance of plurality and difference in the Catholic Church. Pluriformity in unity is presumably the only formula for the future, not only from a social perspective, but also for religion and the Church.

*Translated by John Bowden*

## Notes

1. c. 216: 'No undertaking shall assume the name "Catholic" unless the consent of the competent ecclesiastical authority is given.' c. 300: 'No association shall assume the

name "Catholic" without the consent of competent ecclesiastical authority, in accord with the norm of can. 312.' c. 803 §3: 'Even if it really be Catholic, no school may bear the title Catholic school without the consent of the competent ecclesiastical authority.' c. 808: 'Even if it really be Catholic, no university may bear the title or name *Catholic university* without the consent of the competent ecclesiastical authority.'

2. This states: '*Nullum autem inceptum nomen catholicum sibi vindicet, nisi consensus accesserit legitimae auctoritatis ecclesiasticae.*' (No work may be called Catholic without the assent of the competent church authority.)

3. *Magnopere curandum est, ut id teneamus, quod ubique, quod semper, quod ab omnibus creditum est, hoc est enim vere proprieque catholicum.*

4. The Dutch word 'beleid' is almost impossible to translate into other languages. It means something like programme, policy, or the official leadership of an institution.

5. J. A. van der Ven, *Ecclesiology in Context*, Kampen 1993, 78f., 135ff.

6. *Spring and Autumn of Lu Bu We* XV, 8.

7. Thus for example Eugen Drewermann says that 'in Europe and North America Catholicism no longer corresponds to the culture of interpersonal human relations.'

8. According to Leibniz, no two things in the world are identical. So far, Catholic ecclesiology has not reflected at all on how intrinsically problematical the concept of identity is.

9. c. 205: 'Those baptized are fully in communion with the Catholic Church on this earth who are joined with Christ in its visible structure by the bonds of profession of faith, of the sacraments and of ecclesiastical governance.'

10. Karl Rahner gave splendid expression to this ongoing problem: 'The Church must have a tangible unity in cult, law and faith. But how that is possible along with respect for the very deep differences between the different cultures is a question which has yet to be solved. Today we are asking about a pluralism in theologies, are recognizing such pluralism. In principle we grant, though of course Rome keeps putting on the brake, that there can be and must be different great regional churches, that there can be different liturgies, and finally even that for all the ultimate unity in church law there can be very great differences in the law of the individual particular churches' ('Austausch statt Einbahn. Ritenstreit – neue Aufgaben für die Kirche', *Entschluss/Offen* 38, 1983, 7/8, 28).

# Keep Quiet about Women in the Church

(with apologies to I Corinthians 14.34)

On 22 May 1994 the Holy Father wrote an 'apostolic letter' to his brothers in the episcopate to inform them that there must be an end to the fuss over the possibility of ordaining women to the priesthood. At least that is how I understand the penultimate sentence of this letter: 'Finally to remove any doubt about a question of great importance which concerns the divine constitution of the church, on the basis of my task of strengthening my brethren (cf. Luke 22.32), I affirm that the church is in no way authorized to bestow the priesthood on women and that all believers in the church must regard this standpoint as definitive.'

I think that it is inappropriate to leave the indignation over this letter to women. That would be an implicit confirmation of the opposition in the church between men and women and of the place which men have assigned to women in the church: apart from women servers at mass, who have just been legalized – on the left-hand side of the nave, at a reading for a moment behind the ambo, but certainly not in the sanctuary. So I have not entrusted the writing of this column to a woman, though a woman would certainly have been more competent to write it.

I can imagine many reasons why the Holy Father should think it wise at this moment to deny priestly ordination to women. Indeed I myself would also see a number of these reasons as major objections, though I am not sure whether I would find the objections decisive. However, that does not apply to the reason which the letter gives: Jesus appointed only males as apostles, when he was completely free to have chosen women had he so wished.

This argument indirectly touches on my sphere of professional competence, that of New Testament scholarship. Indirectly, since it is based on something which never happened and is not written or written about anywhere in the New Testament. This remarkable feature has led in my circles to sharp jibes like: 'Jesus also appointed only Jews to be apostles . . .' If such a jibe were made by an outsider, I would primarily feel insulted, and I am inclined to think it unfair and inappropriate. But after that I feel deeply ashamed, because it infallibly shows up the weakness of the argument.

The differences between men and women are certainly of a completely different nature from those between Jews and Gentiles, but in Gal. 3.28 Paul said that not only the difference between male and female, between slave and free, but also that between Jew and Gentile is irrelevant for faith. That gives the joke a certain degree of justification. But even outside this summary of Paul's one can also extend the list of people whom Jesus did not choose to be apostles by an infinite number of varieties. It will strike a biblical scholar, for example, that no scribe is called to be an apostle, though the Gospel mentions a scribe who is not far from the kingdom of God (Mark 12.34). And as for ordinations to the priesthood, it is striking that not a single levite or priest is to be found among the apostles, indeed that while a tax-collector by the name of Levi is certainly called by Jesus to follow him (Mark 2.14), he does not appear in the list of the twelve apostles (Mark 3.16–19), while Jesus is unmistakably said to have been the friend of tax-collectors and sinners (Matt. 11.19; Luke 7.34).

Finally, the jibe uncovers a deeper problem to which no one, so far as I know, has drawn attention. This is the philosophical question whether one can ever rightly prove a statement from something which has not happened or is not written or described anywhere. I am not a trained philosopher, and so in that respect I have not had as professional a schooling as the Holy Father himself. But I humbly ask myself whether there is not a great philosophical problem here on which – if he does not find the suggestion impertinent – he might perhaps reflect once again on the basis of his philosophical competence.

However, that is only half the problem. The other half concerns the putting an end to the discussion, which moreover is to apply to 'all the faithful of the church'. Now the Holy Father may mean this to apply to all the faithful of the Roman Catholic church, but even that already raises great difficulties. I am under the impression that the church hitherto has exercised clear rules according to which '*Roma locuta, causa finita*' has been given certain clearly defined limits.

My understanding is that the fact that this statement by the Holy Father does not stand in an 'apostolic constitution', but only in a letter, is reason enough to infer that it cannot really be binding. We are therefore surprised by a binding statement in a non-binding document. Here I cannot get out of my head the image of the famous hair with which Baron Münchausen got himself out of the bog. One truly does not need to suffer from what for convenience I shall simply call an 'authority neurosis' to pigeonhole the letter – with all due respect for the Holy Father – a letter which also once again passes over all the serious publications on this subject which have appeared over the last decade – as one of those embarrassing letters which are sometimes sent.

It is not unusual for less holy fathers also to tell their children to stop squabbling. That almost never does any good. On the contrary, understanding mothers try to tell the fathers to keep calm. But they never do. And that will always be the case.

Bas van Iersel

*The editors of the Special Column are Norbert Greinacher and Bas van Iersel. The content of the Special Column does not necessarily reflect the views of the Editorial Board of* Concilium.

# Contributors

NORBERT GREINACHER was born in Freiberg im Breisgau in 1931. After studies in Freiburg, Paris and Vienna he gained his doctorate in theology in 1955. Since 1969 he has been Professor of Practical Theology in the Catholic Theological Faculty of the University of Tübingen. His publications include: *Soziologie der Pfarrei*, Freiburg 1955; *Die Kirche in der städtischen Gesellschaft*, Mainz 1966; *Einführung in die Praktische Theologie*, Munich 1976; *Gelassene Leidenschaft*, Zurich 1977; *Gemeindepraxis. Analysen und Aufgaben*, Munich 1979; *Der Fall Küng. Eine Dokumentation*, Munich 1980; *Freiheitsrechte für Christen?*, Munich 1980; *Christsein als Beruf*, Zurich 1981; *Im Angesicht meiner Feinde – Mahl des Friedens*, Gütersloh 1982; *El Salvador – Massaker im Namen der Freiheit*, Hamburg 1982; *Der Konflikt um die Theologie der Befreiung*, Munich ³1985; *Umkehr und Neubeginn*, Fribourg CH 1986; *Katholische Kirche – Wohin?* (with Hans Küng), Munich 1986; *Menschlich Leben*, Zurich 1986; *Der Schrei nach Gerechtigkeit*, Munich 1986; *Leidenschaft für die Armen*, Munich 1990; *Der pastorale Notstand*, Düsseldorf 1992.

Address: Ahornweg 4, D70726 Tübingen, Germany.

JAMES H. PROVOST is a priest of the diocese of Helena, Montana, and a professor of canon law at The Catholic University of America, where he also chairs the Department of Canon Law. He was born in 1939 and was ordained at the American College in Louvain, Belgium in 1963, after completing theological studies at the University of Louvain. In 1967 he received a doctorate in canon law from the Lateran University in Rome. He serves as managing editor of *The Jurist*. He is a past president of the Canon Law Society of America, and served as its Executive Coordinator from 1980 to 1986. He is one of the directors for the Church Order section of *Concilium*.

Address: Department of Canon Law, The Catholic University of America, Washington, DC 20064, USA.

JOHANNES A. VAN DER VEN was born in 1940; he is Professor of Pastoral

Theology at the Catholic University of Nijmegen, and head of the research programme RECOMET (Religious Communication in an Empirical Theology). His publications include: *Katechetische leerplanontwikkeling*, Den Bosch 1973; *Kritische godsdienstdidactiek*, Kampen 1982; *Vorming in waarden en normen*, Kampen 1985; *Pastoraal tussen ideal en werkelijkheid*, Kampen 1985; *Practical Theology. An Empirical Approach*, Kampen 1993; *Ecclesiology in Context*, Grand Rapids and Kampen 1994.

   Address: Katholieke Universiteit, Theologische Faculteit, Postbus 9103, 6500 HD Nijmegen, Netherlands.

GEOFFREY KING was born in Sydney, Australia, in 1943. He entered the Society of Jesus in 1960 and was ordained priest in 1973. He studied history at the University of Melbourne, and obtained a doctorate in canon law from the Catholic University of America in 1979. From 1979 to 1989 he lectured in canon law and church history in the United Faculty of Theology, an ecumenical faculty in Melbourne, Australia. He is currently Director of the East Asian Pastoral Institute, Quezon City, Philippines.

   Address: East Asian Pastoral Institute, Ateneo de Manila University, PO Box 221, 1101 U P Campus QC, Philippines.

ALPHONSE BORRAS was born in Liège in 1951 and was ordained priest in the diocese in 1976. A licenciate in theology and a Doctor in Canon Law of the Gregorian University, he is now professor of ecclesiology and canon law in the Major Seminary in Liège. He also teaches canon law in the Jesuit Institute of Theological Studies and at the Centre for Theological and Pastoral Studies in Brussels. A specialist in penal canon law, he has written two authoritative books in this sphere: *L'excommunication dans le nouveau code de droit canonique. Essai de définition*, Paris 1987; *Les sanctions dans l'Église. Commentaire des canons 1311–1399*, Paris 1990. He has also written numerous articles on canon law and pastoral theology.

   Address: Rue de Prémontrés 40, B 4000 Liège, Belgium.

ERNEST HENAU was born in Erwetegem, Belgium. He entered the Passionists in 1956 and was ordained priest in 1963, then gaining his doctorate in theology in 1967 at the Catholic University of Louvain. From 1969 he has taught in the theological faculties of Louvain, Tilburg and Heerlen. Between 1975 and 1976 he had a Humboldt grant to work at the University of Würzburg. He is now director of Flemish radio and television in Brussels and Professor of Pastoral Theology at the Catholic University of Nijmegen. His major publications are: *Waarom Kerk?* (1974); *Inleiding tot de praktische Homiletiek* (1976); *Verscheidenheid in kerkbetrokkenheid* (1982); *Zaaien op asfalt?* (1991)? *God op de buis* (1993).

Address: Mechelsesteenweg 82, B 1970 Wezembeek-Oppem, Belgium.

NORBERT METTE was born in Barkhausen/porta, Germany in 1946. After studying theology and sociology he gained a doctorate in theology, and since 1984 he has been Professor of Practical Theology at the University of Paderborn. He is married with three children, and is an Editorial Director of *Concilium*. He has written numerous works on pastoral theology and religious education, including: *Voraussetzungen christlicher Elementarerziehung*, Düsseldorf 1983; *Kirche auf dem Weg ins Jahr 2000* (with M. Blasberg-Kuhnke), Düsseldorf 1986; *Gemeindepraxis in Grundbegriffen* (with C. Bäumler), Munich and Düsseldorf 1987; *Auf der Seite der Unterdrückten? Theologie der Befreiung im Kontext Europas* (ed. with P. Eicher), Düsseldorf 1989; *Der Pastorale Notstand* (with O. Fuchs), Düsseldorf 1992.

Address: Liebigweg 11a, D 48165 Münster, Germany.

ROCH PAGÉ is a priest in the diocese of Chicoutimi, Quebec, Canada, where he was born in 1939. After his licence in canon law at the Gregorian University, he gained his doctorate at St Paul University, Canada, in 1968. From 1969 he was in charge of the spiritual training of the future priests in his diocese, and since then he has taught at the Faculty of Canon Law of St Paul University, where he is a professor. His writings – among others on *Les Eglises particulières* (2 vols.) – are for the most part on the law relating to dioceses, but also on the associations of the faithful, which he teaches, and on procedural and matrimonial law. Articles include 'Associations of the Faithful in the Church', *The Jurist*, 47, 1989; 'Le document sur la profession de foi et le serment de fidélité', *Studia canonica* 24, 1990; 'Juges laics et exercice du pouvoir judiciaire', in *Unico Ecclesiae servitio*, Ottawa 1991; 'Les synodes diocésains', in *L'année canonique* II, 1992.

Address: Université Saint-Paul, 223, rue Main, Ottawa ON, K1S 1CS, Canada.

ROBERT D. DUGGAN is a priest of the Archdiocese of Washington DC, where he currently serves as pastor of a parish. He holds a Licence in Sacred Theology from the Gregorian University (Rome) and a Doctorate in Sacred Theology from the Catholic University of America (Washington, DC). His publications include *The Christian Initiation of Children*, New York 1991 (with Maureen A. Kelly); *The Catholic Faith Inventory*, New York 1986 (with Kenneth Boyack and Paul Heusing); and

*Conversion and the Catechumenate*, New York 1984. He has written and spoken extensively on sacramental and liturgical issues, both from a scholarly and a pastoral perspective.

Address: 11811 Clopper Road, Gaithersburg, MD 20878, USA.

DAVID TRACY was born in 1939 in Yonkers, New York. He is a priest of the diocese of Bridgeport, Connecticut, and a doctor of theology of the Gregorian University, Rome. He is the Greeley Distinguished Service Professor of Philosophical Theology at the Divinity School of Chicago University. He is the author of *The Achievement of Bernard Lonergan* (1970), *Blessed Rage for Order: New Pluralism in Theology* (1975), *The Analogical Imagination* (1980), and *Plurality and Ambiguity* (1987).

Address: University of Chicago, Divinity School/Swift Hall, 1025 East 58th Street, Chicago, Ill. 60637, USA.

ANDRÉ BIRMELÉ is Professor of Systematic Theology in the University of Human Sciences, Strasbourg; he also works in the Centre of Ecumenical Studies of the World Lutheran Federation in Strasbourg, a role which makes him a particpant in numerous national, European and international ecumenical dialogues. He was a member of the Faith and Order Commission between 1984 and 1991, and since 1991 has been the French representative on the Central Committee of the World Council of Churches. In addition to numerous articles, his main works are *Le salut en Jésus Christ dans les dialogues oecuméniques*, Paris 1986; *La foi des Eglises luthériennes* (with Marc Lienhard), Paris 1991; *Grundkonsens-Grunddifferenz* (with Harding Meyer), Frankfurt and Paderborn 1992.

Address: Centres d'Etudes Oecuméniques, 8 rue Gustave Klotz, 67000 Strasbourg, France.

KNUT WALF was born in Berlin-Dahlem in 1936. After studying philosophy, theology, law and canon law in Munich and Fribourg, in 1962 he was ordained priest in West Berlin. He gained his doctorate in canon law at the University of Munich in 1965, and between 1966 and 1968 was a pastor in West Berlin. After his Habilitation in Munich in 1971, from 1972–1977 he lectured in church and state church law in Munich, where he was also Director of the Canonistic Institute. Since 1977 he has been Professor of Canon Law in the Catholic University of Nijmegen and since 1985 has also been Professor in the Theological Faculty in Tilburg, The Netherlands. More recent publications on church law and theology are: *Menschenrechte in der Kirche*, Düsseldorf 1980; *Stille Fluchten – Zur Veränderung des religiösen Bewusstseins*, Munich 1983; *Einführung in das neue katholische Kirchenrecht*, Zürich, Einsiedeln and Cologne 1984; *Kirchenrecht*, Düsseldorf 1984; *Vragen rondom het nieuwe kerkelijk recht*, Hilversum 1988; *Western Bibliography of Taoism*, Essen [3]1992; *Tao für den Westen – eine Hinführung*, Munich 1989. He is regularly involved in *Orientierung*, Zurich.

Address: Bart Hendriksstraat 17, NL 6523 RE Nijmegen, Netherlands.

# Members of the Advisory Committee for Canon Law

*Directors*

| | | |
|---|---|---|
| James Provost | Washington DC | United States |
| Knut Walf | Nijmegen | Netherlands |

*Members*

| | | |
|---|---|---|
| Philippe Antoine | Bamako | Republic of Mali |
| Frederico Aznar Gil | Salamanca | Spain |
| Mme Basdevant-Gaudemet | Sceaux | France |
| William Bassett | San Francisco | United States |
| Jean Bernhard | Strasbourg | France |
| Giovanni Cereti | Rome | Italy |
| James Coriden | Silver Spring, MA | United States |
| Antonio García y García | Salamanca | Spain |
| Jean Gaudemet | Paris | France |
| Thomas Green | Washington, DC | United States |
| Joseph Hajjar | Damascus | Syria |
| Peter Huizing SJ | Nijmegen | Netherlands |
| Ruud Huysmans | Voorburg | Netherlands |
| Geoffrey King SJ | Manila | Philippines |
| Michel Legrain | Paris | France |
| Klaus Lüdicke | Münster | Germany |
| Julio Manzanares | Salamanca | Spain |
| Elizabeth McDonough OP | Washington, DC | United States |
| Francis Morrissey OMI | Ottawa, Ont. | Canada |
| Hubert Müller | Bonn | Germany |
| Rik Torfs | Louvain | Belgium |
| Myriam Wijlens | Münster | Germany |
| Francesco Zanchini | Rome | Italy |

*Directors/Counsellors—cont.*

| | | |
|---|---|---|
| | Münster | Germany |
| | Tübingen | Germany |
| | Tübingen | Germany |
| Johann-Baptist Metz | Gonawala-Kelaniya | Sri Lanka |
| Dietmar Mieth | Washington, DC | USA |
| Jürgen Moltmann | Nijmegen | The Netherlands |
| Aloysius Pieris SJ | Paris | France |
| James Provost | Budapest | Hungary |
| Edward Schillebeeckx | Chicago, IL | USA |
| Christoph Theobald SJ | Madrid | Spain |
| Miklós Tomka | Nijmegen | The Netherlands |
| David Tracy | Athens | Greece |
| Marciano Vidal CSSR | | |
| Knut Walf | | |
| Christos Yannaras | | |

General Secretariat: Prins Bernardstraat 2, 6521 AB Nijmegen, The Netherlands
Manager: Mrs E. C. Duindam-Deckers

# Concilium

## Issues of *Concilium* to be published in 1995

### 1995/1: The Bible as Cultural Heritage

*Edited by Giuseppe Alberigo, Wim Beuken and Sean Freyne*

Focusses on the Bible as a cultural rather than religious inheritance. First, it looks at the function of the Bible as a window on the Ancient Near East. Then it shows how the Bible has found a place in various fields of traditional culture. Finally, it examines the Bible in the context of cross-cultural and cross-disciplinary study.

*030030 7    February*

### 1995/2: The Many Faces of the Divine

*Edited by Hermann Häring and Johann Baptist Metz*

God is believed in, experienced and responded to in many ways. How can the one tradition be enriched by the insights of others without the disintegration of all traditions? What is at stake in belief in God? These are the questions tackled in this issue.

*030031 5    April*

### 1995/3: Liturgy and the Body

*Edited by Louis Chauvet and François Kabasele Lumbala*

This issue begins by considering the use of the body and the senses in liturgy; it then moves on to the relationship between the liturgy, the body and corporate memory; finally it looks at current problems raised by a more physical liturgy in modern society.

*030032 3    June*

## 1995/4: The Family

*Edited by Lisa Sowle Cahill and Dietmar Mieth*

Do the Bible and Christian tradition advance a particular form or forms of the family? How do they place the family in relation to religious commitment? What resources does Christianity provide for a reconsideration of the roles of family members, a critique of unjust relationships and a spirituality or theology of the family?

*03033 1    August*


## 1995/5: Poverty and Ecology

*Edited by Leonardo Boff and Aloysius Pieris*

*03034 X    October*


## 1995/6: Religion and Naturalism

*Edited by John Coleman and Miklós Tomka*

*03035 8    December*


## Issues to be Published in 1996

# Concilium Subscription Information – outside North America

**Individual** Annual Subscription (six issues): £30.00

**Institution** Annual Subscription (six issues): £40.00

**Airmail** subscriptions: add £10.00

Individual issues: £8.95 each

---

**New** subscribers please return this form:
for a two-year subscription, double the appropriate rate

(for individuals)     £30.00     (1/2 years)        . . . .

(for institutions)     £40.00     (1/2 years)        . . . .

Airmail postage
outside Europe +£10.00     (1/2 years)        . . . .

                                    **Total** . . . . . . . .

I wish to subscribe for one/two years as an individual/institution
(delete as appropriate)

Name/Institution . . . . . . . . . . . . . . . . . . . . . . . . . . . . . . . . . . .

Address . . . . . . . . . . . . . . . . . . . . . . . . . . . . . . . . . . . . . . . . .

. . . . . . . . . . . . . . . . . . . . . . . . . . . . . . . . . . . . . . . . . . . .

. . . . . . . . . . . . . . . . . . . . . . . . . . . . . . . . . . . . . . . . . . . .

I enclose a cheque for ...................... payable to SCM Press Ltd

Please charge my Access/Visa/Mastercard no.   . . . . . . . . . . . . . . . .

Signature . . . . . . . . . . . . . . . . . . . . . . .Expiry Date . . . . . . . . .

Please return this form to:
**SCM PRESS LTD 26-30 Tottenham Road, London N1 4BZ**